BIG BROTHER
and the
GRIM REAPER

BIG BROTHER

and the

GRIM REAPER

Political Life After Death

BENJAMIN GINSBERG

MICHIGAN STATE UNIVERSITY PRESS | *East Lansing*

Michigan State University Press
East Lansing, Michigan 48823-5245

Library of Congress Cataloging-in-Publication Data
Names: Ginsberg, Benjamin, author.
Title: Big Brother and the Grim Reaper : political life after death / Benjamin Ginsberg.
Description: East Lansing : Michigan State University Press, 2024. | Includes bibliographical references and index.
Identifiers: LCCN 2024015050 | ISBN 9781611865127 (cloth) | ISBN 9781611865080 (paperback)
| ISBN 9781609177690 | ISBN 9781628955293
Subjects: LCSH: Death—Political aspects. | Thanatology—Political aspects. |
Secularism—Political aspects. | Memorialization—Political aspects.
Classification: LCC HQ1073 .G55 2024 | DDC 306.9—dc23/eng/20240422
LC record available at https://lccn.loc.gov/2024015050

Cover design by David Drummond, Salamander Design, www.salamanderhill.com

Visit Michigan State University Press at www.msupress.org

For Sandy

Acknowledgments

wish to thank my editor Elizabeth Demers for her advice and support. In addition, many thanks to project editor Anastasia Wraight, copyeditor Deborah Oosterhouse, Liz Deegan, Nicole Utter, and Terika Hernandez.

Contents

The Thanatotic Contract

eath is the dark matter of politics; it pervades the political universe but is poorly understood. Most people fear death, their own as well as that of loved ones, and will do what they can to hide from the Grim Reaper.[1] To some, the dead may seem inert, lifeless, lacking in potency. The dead, however, have always possessed power. At one time, this power was metaphysical and spiritual. Today, however, the dead also exercise secular power sometimes, through the courts. At one time, fear of death strengthened religious institutions. Today, dread of the Dark Angel mainly bolsters the power of the state.[2] As we shall see, death binds rulers and ruled in a thanatotic contract that promises the ruled eternal life within the embrace of the nation while offering rulers the immortality of fame. At one time, immortality was a gift (or a curse) from the gods. Today, life and death are secular matters. Immortality can be a gift (or a curse) from the state.

Efforts to regulate death have become an important source of power for states and secular rulers. States hope to secure popular loyalty and obedience by extending citizens' lives, promising to effectuate the postmortem fulfillment of citizens' antemortem desires, and offering ersatz forms of immortality for the truly deserving. In essence, Big Brother has sought to benefit from befriending and domesticating the Grim Reaper.

To begin our exploratory excursion into the realm of death, let us remember that death is a political and social as well as a biological phenomenon. Everywhere, the risks and causes of death are influenced by laws and policies, to say nothing of the violent political struggles that produce large numbers of deaths every year. States as well as their allies and adversaries endeavor to control populations or, as Achille Mbembe puts it, to "subjugate" life by threatening or meting out death to their foes.[3] The role of death in the political realm, though, is more complex than killing or its threat. States not only vow death to their enemies, but like many religions they also hold out promises of salvation or even immortality to their adherents. And, like the church, the state treats the loyal dead with respect, sometimes offering them a place in the secular afterlife of honor and memory, while consigning the faithless to the void.

States are sometimes thought to exercise power only over the lands of the living. Michel Foucault wrote that death was the "borderline between two sovereignties—earthly and heavenly."[4] Some are anxious to flee across this metaphysical borderline to seek refuge from the power of the state. Consider, among many famous examples, the Sicarii said to have killed themselves in 73 AD to escape from the Roman legion that breached the walls of the fortress of Masada after a lengthy siege during the First Jewish-Roman War. Or, for that matter, remember the tragic case of Weimar social critic Walter Benjamin, who chose to escape the German state by using enough morphine to secure his passage across the notional border of the kingdom of death when the national borders of France and Spain provided insufficient safety from the *Gestapo*.

In a more religious world, faith, prayer, and spiritual leaders offered a hope of protection in this life and immortality in the next. In many cultures the rituals surrounding death and the proper disposition of the remains are needed to ensure decedents a smooth passage to eternity and to dissuade the dead from harboring any resentment toward the living.[5] Religious institutions derived considerable earthly influence from their power over death and a hoped-for afterlife.[6]

In the more secular present, however, states have elbowed religious bodies aside from many matters involving death and dying. States have crossed Foucault's metaphysical borderline and launched incursions into the dark realm. In Foucauldian terms, we might say that the state has bureaucratized death to strengthen its power over life. States and political leaders not only offer to protect their loyal citizens from death; they promise an immortality said to come with membership in a nation. While nations are not truly immortal, most are more enduring than individuals, offering those who surrender to the nation's embrace at least some hope of delay before final oblivion.

For those they favor, states also create an afterlife from which the dead may continue to exercise rights and influence in the world of the living and receive posthumous honors as rewards. Those dubious about the idea of posthumous rights and influence might familiarize themselves with the contemporary legal concept of the testamentary trust or consider the much older examples of the Inca mummies. The mummified corpses of deceased Inca emperors continued to own property and, with just a bit of help from members of the noble *panaqa*, were able to make posthumous decisions about its disposition.[7]

On the other hand, for those they disfavor, states sometimes offer not only death but also oblivion. Some unfortunates are thrown into mass graves and others buried anonymously in potter's fields like New York's Hart Island, the resting place of over a million poorly identified corpses. But, as we shall see, politics is complicated, and in the political realm death, and even oblivion, are not necessarily permanent. Resurrection—at least political rebirth—is possible.

The Thanatotic Contract

At the heart of every state is a thanatotic contract between rulers and ruled. Each depends upon the other for immortality. The ruled are promised immortality in the bosom of the nation. Rulers, for their part, seek the immortality of fame. Several of America's founders saw fame as the pathway to eternal life.

Individuals will do many things to lessen their dread of death. As Martin Heidegger noted, many even avoid contact with dying persons as though the act of dying is something against which individuals should be guarded.[8] A similar point was made by Norbert Elias who wrote that "ageing" and "old age" have become almost taboo terms in Western societies because they remind individuals of the inevitability of death.[9] For millennia, the fear of death has given rise to superstitions, cults, and religions that promise an afterlife or life on some alternate plane to faithful adherents. But where religious belief has waned, citizens will often look to secular political leaders for protection. During the coronavirus crisis, millions watched national leaders on television, hoping that these individuals could shield them from the plague. Their own fear of death, in turn, leads these selfsame political leaders to look to their followers to help them achieve immortality.

Many political leaders espouse ideologies like various forms of nationalism, communism, fascism, and even democracy, whose value transcends death. Indeed, political leaders often mobilize their followers by telling them that failure to achieve a goal is worse than death. Take Patrick Henry's fiery speech at the 1775 Virginia convention. Henry famously declared, "Give me liberty or give me death." In other words, the loss of liberty was to be feared more than death. The notion of something worth dying for, be it liberty, honor, victory, the nation, the revolution, or some other putatively transcendent value, is an idea from which individuals can take great comfort. This idea derates death to a secondary concern, perhaps stripping away some of the terror from the threat of personal extinction.

Moreover, by offering them followership—the modern-day equivalent of holy communion—leaders offer their acolytes a powerful form of self-transcendence through a collective immortality they could not hope to achieve as mere individuals.[10] Hitler made frequent and effective use of this idea. He was fond of declaring that the Third Reich would live for a thousand years. In this way, Hitler offered

Germans the promise of near immortality if they surrendered their individuality and submerged themselves in the nation under his leadership. Mao Zedong similarly declared that revolutionary China was "eternal and indestructible."[11] The Third Reich is no longer with us, but China seems alive and well despite the tens of millions of corpses left by Mao and his lieutenants.

The fear of death and search for immortality are important elements in the power of nationalism. Individuals are able to hide from death as followers within the nominally immortal nation. Robert J. Lifton referred to this type of belief as a sense of "symbolic immortality," providing individuals with the sense that they are part of an enduring entity that transcends their own mortality.[12] In this vein, Nobel Prize–winning Polish poet Czeslaw Milosz observed that as individuals lose faith in God and their belief in individual immortality, they are drawn to the idea of collective immortality.[13] Similarly, in their discussion of ethnonational struggles in the Balkans in recent decades, Milovan R. Subotić and Miroslav Mitrović observe that a factor contributing to the rise of competing Balkan nationalisms is a "longing for immortality" leading individuals to submerge themselves in their separate and mutually hostile nations.[14] Quite a number of experimental studies reviewed by Sheldon Solomon and Sharlynn Thompson have also concluded that a sense of belonging to an enduring nation headed by a powerful leader provides individuals with a sense of symbolic immortality and lessens their fear of death.[15]

Ironically, this longing for immortality has helped to fuel bloody struggles as faithful citizens demonstrated their willingness to die and kill for the nation. These individual deaths, however, nominally contribute to the immortality of the nation and so are said to be welcomed rather than feared. In Johann Wilhelm Kleist's nineteenth-century "Prussian War Songs," death for the fatherland is said not only to be a duty and a privilege but to "open the gate to immortality."[16] This idea that individual death was to be welcomed as it contributed to the longevity of the nation was echoed during the Nazi period when Schutzstaffel (SS) troopers were taught not to fear their own deaths because these "nourished" the life of the nation.[17]

The longevity of the nation, moreover, was preserved by killing its foes. Similar views can be found among leaders of contemporary radical groups that make use of suicide bombings to achieve their goals. Hezbollah leader Hasan Nasrallah declared, "We are going to win because they love life and we love death."[18] In his 1930 study, Maurice Halbwachs argued that self-extinction undertaken "within the bosom of the community" and to preserve its existence should be termed a sacrifice rather than a suicide to emphasize the fact that the act's purpose was to preserve rather than extinguish life.[19] In some respects, nationalism democratizes immortality. As Baudrillard observes, immortality was once seen as an emblem of power and only available to ruling elites. Today, immortality is available to followers as well as rulers.[20]

Followership, moreover, provides individuals with an opportunity to shelter behind heroic figures who will protect them from death and evil. In past eras, leaders claimed or were deemed to possess mystical powers, including the power to overcome death. Thus, according to his disciples, Jesus conquered death and rose from his tomb. This mastery of death putatively demonstrated that Jesus had the power to save his followers from the terrors of the grave.[21] In the modern era, secular leaders—Abraham Lincoln, Winston Churchill, Charles de Gaulle, Joseph Stalin, and others—were called or depicted themselves as saviors suggesting that, like Jesus, they possessed power over death, and the ability to prevent the deaths of their nations.[22] In the Soviet media, Stalin was often portrayed as the savior not only of his own nation but of all Europe.

Often, the deification of leaders requires quite a bit of rewriting of history. North Korea has taken official revision of history to a new extreme. In 2013, after paramount leader Kim Jong-un executed his uncle and former vice premier, Jang Song Thaek, Mr. Jang's name and photo were expunged from all official accounts and documents. It seemed that he had never existed. Subsequently, North Korea proceeded to erase 99 percent of its official news archive. Only articles published since the ascension of Kim Jong-un and a small number of laudatory articles published about Kim before he took power were retained. As a result, North Korea's official history now appears to begin with the current Mr. Kim.[23] How could anyone doubt Kim's heroic stature or his ability to preserve the life of the nation?

Unfortunately, propaganda may not be enough to convince citizens of their leaders' heroic stature. Often, secular leaders may feel compelled to demonstrate their power over death by destroying their foes and spilling their blood. By wielding death, leaders affirm to their followers that they possess power over the Dark Angel and, hence, the power to protect others from it. Those who possess the power to dispense death also possess the power to protect life.[24] Achilles dragged the body of Hector behind his chariot before the walls of Troy to demonstrate his power to wield death to his foes, and so his power to preserve the lives of his followers. Aztec rulers sacrificed enormous numbers of captives in blood-drenched ceremonies because the lifeblood of captured warriors was said to be needed to feed the sun and prevent the destruction of the world.[25] Their power to spill blood literally gave Aztec chiefs the power to prolong life.

The idea of leaders as heroes is echoed in the iconography surrounding political leaders—the portraits and busts—as well as the wailing and other conspicuous displays of grief when a beloved ruler dies.[26] The death of the leader suddenly makes followers vulnerable to the Grim Reaper.[27] Deceased leaders' tombs and monuments are often maintained as great public shrines so that citizens may be assured of a revered leader's continued protection. Vladimir Lenin's tomb comes to mind as an example, as do the Washington and Lincoln Monuments.

Finally, leaders often endeavor to create fetishes that, as Ernest Becker put it, locate the threat to their followers' lives in "some special places where it can be placated and controlled."[28] Among the most famous literary examples of a death fetish was, of course, Moby Dick. For Ahab, pursuit of the white whale was an effort to confront and defeat his own death. The fetishization of death and evil are common in the political world. For Hitler, the Jews, as for Donald Trump, "illegal" immigrants, became fetishes whose destruction would overcome evil and death. In his speeches, Trump pointed to the many Americans allegedly killed by illegals, suggesting that the pursuit and deportation of "criminal aliens" would save American lives.

Hitler's fetishization of the Jews is especially marked. Jews had, of course, lived in Germany for centuries and made substantial contributions to German science, German industry, and German culture. Indeed, Jews had been instrumental in the unification of modern Germany and the construction of the German state. Now, Jews were portrayed as enemies of the German people, cunning swindlers, sexual perverts, and so forth who must be extruded from German society and eventually destroyed to save the nation. Like some modern-day Ahab, Hitler was willing to sacrifice everything— and lead millions of credulous Germans—in his pursuit of a fetish.

How else to explain Hitler's wartime willingness to divert scarce resources to a herculean effort to murder Jews? Throughout the war, Germany devoted substantial resources that were badly needed by its military forces to the campaign against the Jews. The Germans built some ten thousand concentration camps to imprison and murder Jews along with other putative racial enemies. Despite the fact that German military manpower was stretched to its extreme limits, more than one hundred thousand soldiers and military police officers, as well as tens of thousands of civilian officials, were assigned to the task of rounding up, incarcerating, and killing Jews. Trains, trucks, and supplies badly needed by the military were used, instead, to facilitate the transport and murder of Jews. Even as the German army was being driven back by the Soviets, trucks and trains transporting Jews to death camps were given priority over military transports. Like Aztec rulers who thought the blood of their captives must be spilled to preserve the life of their people, Hitler assigned a lower priority to his mundane military effort than to what amounted to bloody magical rituals.

The idea of fetishization also helps to explain why so many Americans are easily attracted to an understanding of domestic politics—most often a sordid and trivial affair—as a Manichean struggle in which life itself is at stake. In the political arena, the

Dark Angel, personified as some petty politician, can be defeated and death forestalled. Take the views expressed by a 2020 website dedicated to the defeat of Donald Trump. "Could Trump be the Antichrist?" the authors ask.

> Prophesy states that no one can ever know for sure, but one thing is certain, most of what comes out of Donald Trump's mouth is quite the opposite of what was said by Jesus. So, he certainly represents values that are opposite to those that were taught by Jesus. Yet, many seem to have accepted Donald Trump as their savior. Preaching violence and non-tolerant behavior is not Christ-like by any stretch of the imagination. In fact, it is juxtaposed.
>
> His quick rise to political power and strange hold over the masses got him elected by the "Christian Coalition." He seems to get away with any and all bad acts relatively unscathed, where most would find themselves jailed or worse. These are but a few of the numerous coincidental facts that have led many to feel that Donald Trump is none other than the Biblical Antichrist![29]

Lest these sentiments seem uniquely related to Trump's foes, it is worth observing that almost every recent president has been fetishized as the personification of evil by some of his opponents. Some declared that Barack Obama was the Antichrist. About 10 percent of U.S. presidents have been murdered by assassins, making the presidency the most dangerous job in the nation.[30] Unfortunately, presidents have become larger-than-life figures, venerated as saviors by some and fetishized as the embodiments of evil and death by others.

The Immortality of Fame

While leaders and rulers offer their followers protection and, perhaps, shelter from death within the immortal nation, these selfsame leaders often pursue a different path to the afterlife for themselves.

In an earlier era, rulers sought to pass on power to their offspring and to dynasties that would keep their names alive through the ages. Today, secular leaders seek to defeat death by achieving and institutionalizing fame and glory. This combination opens the way to a hoped-for path to immortality in a secular afterlife of collective memory and political institutions that, like the pyramids, will stand forever. The term "fame," of course, does not connote the transitory notoriety of the media celebrity but, instead, implies making history and leaving a permanent impression upon the world.

The idea of seeking immortality through fame is not new.[31] In ancient Greece war heroes were rewarded with "imperishable fame." Roman generals, seeking immortality through fame, brought historians and poets along on military expeditions.[32] Similarly, several U.S. presidents, including the late John F. Kennedy, gave sympathetic historians access to their papers, meetings, and decisions in order to burnish their fame. U.S. presidents are often said to seek to accomplish great deeds that would make a mark on history, followed by the enactment of laws and the construction of political institutions that would preserve their legacies.

It was in the eighteenth century that belief in an afterlife waned among educated persons and many became obsessed with posterity, death, and secular paths to immortality.[33] Many of America's founders, including George Washington, Benjamin Franklin, Alexander Hamilton, Samuel Adams, and Thomas Jefferson, had little confidence in the likelihood of a heavenly afterlife but saw fame as a path toward immortality in the afterlife of collective memory. They also believed that participation in the construction of political institutions was the best way to ensure a prominent place in this afterlife.[34]

Several of the founders admired the writings of Francis Bacon whose essay titled "Of Honor and Reputation," originally published in 1597, could be seen as a secular equivalent of the Egyptian *Book of the Dead*. The *Book of the Dead* was actually not a book. This is a term Westerners applied to the collection of spells that purported to offer Egyptian decedents a guide to success and status in the afterlife. Careful study would allow the Egyptian decedent to impress the gods and secure a permanent place in paradise. Similarly, Bacon's essay was understood by the leaders of America's founding generation to offer a guide to success in the secular afterlife of collective memory.[35] Bacon presented a hierarchy or pyramid of fame whose five levels were seen as representations of the likelihood that an individual would earn a secure and desirable spot in the secular afterlife. From the lowest level to the highest these were the following:

1. Those who ruled justly and brought prosperity.
2. Those who enlarged and defended the nation.
3. Those who delivered their country from tyrants.
4. Law givers who governed through their ordinances after they themselves were gone.
5. The founders of states.

The highest and most secure levels of the afterlife—the levels to which both Hamilton and Washington aspired—were reserved for leaders who wrote laws, built institutions, and founded states through which their wills and ideas continued to govern even after their physical bodies had turned to dust. Such individuals secured permanent places in the afterlife by constructing institutions that not only preserved their memories, but carried on the implementation of their ideals as well. Consider that U.S. laws must continue to comport with "the intention of the framers" as expressed in the nation's Constitution. This is the immortality achieved by James Madison, the Constitution's principal author, and his fellow members of the Constitutional Convention.

Friedrich Nietzsche was correct to have Zarathustra call the institutions of the state "cold monsters."[36] These institutions are the quasi-sentient incarnations of the dead. Every state is, in some measure, a thanatocracy. Appropriately enough, these institutional monuments to the dead adiaphorize conduct, effectively sanitizing actions that a living person might find morally abhorrent. Thus, rulers' quest for immortality can drive them to affirm their power over death by spilling the blood of their foes and building monuments to themselves. These bureaucratic monuments, in turn, facilitate or undertake action without regard to its moral content. Is this not the meaning of the phrase "for reason of state"?

In this way, rulers and ruled are signatories to a thanatotic contract. Ordinary individuals follow those whom they hope will provide them with protection from death, while leaders extend such protection to those who, in turn, offer them fame and a passageway to the secular afterlife.

One token of this contract is the treatment of human remains. Diogenes declared that he had no interest in his corpse and advised that when he died, his body could be thrown over the walls of the city to be torn apart by wild beasts. Presumably corpses are indifferent to their treatment, but in every culture most living persons—Diogenes to the contrary notwithstanding—do care how their remains and those of their fellows are treated. Nearly every human culture has evolved rituals and customs that require the respectful treatment of its deceased members.

The level of respect shown to remains may be a function of the decedent's social rank or the honor thought to be due to the decedent. The politically prominent may be accorded elaborate public funerals and impressive tombs. Ordinary individuals are buried not far from one another with small headstones, but the remains of virtuous citizens are treated with respect and legally protected from desecration and dismemberment. Soldiers are entitled to especially dignified military funerals, and enormous efforts are made to recover the bodies of those military men and women killed overseas defending the nation. The military is constantly attempting to recover, identify, and provide proper military funerals for the remains of Americans killed in long-ago wars.[37]

Why do we afford the dead a posthumous right of dignity? The likely answer is that treating the dead with respect is an affirmation of their continuing membership in the nation. The virtuous dead have crossed the border to an honorable afterlife in the bosom of the nation where, as we shall see, they continue to exercise rights and influence. Accordingly, their remains must be treated with proper respect.

Those who are not part of the nation—criminals, rebels, foreign foes—are not entitled to such treatment. The corpses of such persons may be thrown into mass graves or otherwise desecrated. One gruesome example is related by Don Herzog. When the sixteenth-century British soldier Sir Humphrey Gilbert put down a rebellion in Ireland, he disheartened his foes and barred them from the secular afterlife by desecrating the corpses of their dead. "His manner was that the heddes of all those (of what sort soeuer thei were) whiche were killed in the daie, should be cutte of from their bodies . . . and should be laied on the ground . . . the dedde feelying nothyng the more more paines thereby: and yet it did bryng great yerrour to the people, when they saw the heddes of their deddes fathers, brothers, children, kynsfolke and freendes."[38] Thus did the noble Humphrey Gilbert demonstrate that these unworthy dead were not entitled to a place in the afterlife but would be condemned, instead, to some nameless oblivion. By so doing, Gilbert terrified the still-living kinsfolk of the rebels and broke their will to resist.

Unfortunately, this contract between rulers and ruled is often sealed in blood.[39] Aztec, Inca, and Nazi rulers among others demonstrated their power over life and death by wholesale killing. All these groups eventually failed the test of war, and leaders joined their followers in the embrace of death—but not before their dark thanatotic logic led them to drench the ground with blood.

The Secularization of Death

The thanatotic contract is a civil union, not a religious marriage. Rulers and ruled unite before the alter of the state, not before God. This is one aspect of the ongoing secularization of death. At one time, the state governed life, but its power ended with death. For better or worse, the dead passed into a realm beyond the state's reach. The border between the land of the living and that of the dead was guarded by religious institutions that claimed to possess the keys to an afterlife where the souls of the faithful might exist in eternal bliss.

Carl Schmitt observed that the contemporary state has secularized and politicized religious ideas for its own purposes.[1] In this regard, today, it is the state that guards the boundary between life and death. The state has built border outposts and fortifications including the hospital, the coroner's office, and even the secular cemetery where public officials keep watch over the comings and goings of the Dark Angel. From its border outposts, the state works to hold death at bay. At institutions like the U.S. National Institutes of Health, the agents

of the state have deconstructed mortality into its elemental forms
and busily endeavor to defeat death in detail. They seek to conquer
infectious diseases, cancer, heart disease, gun violence, and so forth,
hoping that even if the Dark Angel cannot be confronted directly, it
will be left with an ever dwindling armamentarium.[2]

Contemporary states have even begun to launch forays across
the frontier into the kingdom of death itself, hoping to rescue at
least some of the souls held captive there and to return them to
the world of the living. Contemporary research into the science of
resuscitation is but one example.[3] All these efforts, of course, require
states to undertake heroic exertions and encourage them to greatly
expand their power and capabilities as citizens look to Big Brother
to overcome the Grim Reaper.

State versus Church at Death's Border

In the not too distant past, animistic explanations of disease and
death were generally accepted, and matters related to death, including funerary practices and the interment of remains, were in the hands
of religious bodies. In the West, deaths were recorded in church
records. Prayer and priestly intervention were designed to propitiate
the deity and to offer communities some protection from visits by
the Dark Angel. The sick and dying sought care in monasteries and
other religious institutions such as the French "hotel-Dieux," or
hostel of God, where religious worship had a higher priority than
mundane medical care. And, of course, religious leaders advised
the faithful on the best routes to eternal life. Religious institutions,
indeed, derived much of their earthly power from their presumptive
understanding of death.

In the West, however, belief in a spiritual afterlife has waned,
and many seek to extend their lives in this world, or even to secure
some secular form of immortality. In much of the world, indeed,
the state has taken the regulation of death away from religious
authorities. States have made death a secular and administrative,
more than a religious, matter. They have introduced their own rules

and procedures and have replaced priests and prayer with public health regulations to mitigate the spread of disease and death.

In Europe the transition from religious to state determination of the rules surrounding death could be seen even before the Protestant Reformation weakened the power of the church. These included such innovations as the development of official mortality records in the twelfth century and the public health rules instituted in a number of Italian city-states during the Black Death of the late fourteenth century. In England, when Henry VIII ordered most monasteries closed, municipalities took responsibility for the operation of hospitals. State responsibility for death also became evident in the early nineteenth century when the cemetery began to supplant the church graveyard as the community's chief place of burial. Cemeteries fell under the control of municipal governments, not churches, and were, in particular, governed by public health ordinances designed to prevent the spread of disease.

Today death, including both its prevention and memorialization, has become a major realm of governmental activity and an important source of state power. For example, public health agencies maintain mortality statistics and endeavor to control outbreaks of fatal illnesses. Public safety agencies investigate auto crashes, food toxicities, and product failures and issue rules and recommendations designed to prevent fatalities. The coroner or medical examiner determines causes of death and issues death certificates. The police investigate and endeavor to solve deaths related to criminal activity. Probate courts enforce testamentary rights. And, as I write this page during the U.S. Memorial Day weekend, I note that the state asks us to remember the virtuous dead and to learn from their example. Generally speaking, in the Western world the state has supplanted the church at the border between life and death.

From Churchyard to Cemetery

In Europe before the eighteenth century, the dead were entrusted to the church for safekeeping while they awaited resurrection. Decedents were buried mainly in churchyards—according to the rules and customs of the church. Important members of the aristocracy and members of the clergy might be buried within the church building itself, usually in underground vaults. Some particularly pious individuals preferred the churchyard, believing that only martyrs and especially meritorious persons deserved to be buried within the church.[4] The church undertook to protect the dead entrusted to its care by levying harsh punishments for the desecration of graves and stamping out such pagan customs as dancing on tombs and graves to affirm the joy of life.[5]

The dead, with the exception of suicides, heretics, criminals, and others deemed unworthy, were buried with their heads oriented toward the east so that they would be facing Jerusalem on the day of resurrection. Virtuous individuals were generally buried at the south end of the graveyard and reprobates at the north. Particularly odious persons might be barred from the consecrated ground of the churchyard and buried in a field or even a crossroad. Such individuals would be denied resurrection and their ghosts left to wander for all eternity. Hence the right to be buried in the churchyard was an important one, and the decision as to whether to allow a decedent burial in a particular churchyard and where exactly the grave was to be placed, an important source of power, and sometimes revenue, for priests and other church officials. This power could cause some resentment. A frequently quoted epitaph from an English country church reads:

> Here I lie by the chancel door,
> They put me here because I was poor.
> The further in the more you pay,
> But here I lie as snug as they.[6]

Conflicts could break out when church authorities chose to reject a decedent. This became an important matter during the religious disputes of the seventeenth and eighteenth centuries. In Britain, then divided by sectarian strife, Anglican ministers typically refused burial to Catholics as did Catholic priests to Anglicans. In the Catholic nations of the European continent the church denied burial to Protestants and other heretics. In a number of cases, famous anticlerical writers were forced to make deathbed renunciations of their views in order to be allowed burial in the churchyard. One exception was the Enlightenment philosopher Voltaire. The church had threatened to deny Voltaire burial on church grounds if he did not recant his anti-Catholic views and properly accept Jesus Christ as his savior. Asked on his deathbed by a priest if he would acknowledge Christ's divinity, Voltaire answered, "Do not mention that name to me."[7] Nevertheless, fearing riots and destruction of church property by the philosopher's ardent admirers, church authorities agreed that Voltaire's retort had sufficiently acknowledged Christ to allow the philosopher to be buried on church grounds.

During the eighteenth and nineteenth centuries, the churchyard was gradually supplanted by the cemetery, a secular institution, as the resting ground of the dead. Cemeteries were governed by secular law rather than religious authority, though some cemeteries might have been affiliated with particular faiths. The cemetery was religiously neutral—open to decedents of all faiths, perhaps each in particular sections—and religious authorities could not deny access to their critics. The shift from graveyards to cemeteries as burial sites, moreover, became associated with public health concerns. Graveyards had become overcrowded and the sources of unpleasant odors, and were seen as a threat to public health.[8]

In 1799, for example, Napoleon Bonaparte became perturbed about the dangers to public health associated with Paris's overcrowded graveyards. The then First Counsul announced a competition for the development of new public cemeteries on the outskirts of Paris. The winning design was submitted by architect Alexandre-Théodore Brongniart who proposed a site in the hills outside Paris. After the cemetery was completed, municipal authorities named it Pere Lachaise after Louis XIV's famous Jesuit confessor and sought to make the cemetery more attractive to Parisians by moving the bodies of famous people from their current resting places to the new site. For example, the remains of the famous ill-fated seventeenth-century lovers Heloise and Abelard were moved to a grave marked by a large granite monument near the new cemetery's entrance. This publicity campaign was quite successful, and today more than one million people are buried at Pere Lachaise. This campaign might have been among the earliest examples of the marketing of cemeteries, but such publicity campaigns are commonplace today.[9]

With the emergence of the germ theory of disease, churchyards came to be viewed as places where contagion festered and spread, and churchyard burials fell from favor. The new public cemeteries were usually built in the countryside, away from population centers. Cemeteries, moreover, were and are regulated by municipal health and sanitation ordinances that promised to prevent the dead from posing a danger to the living. Religious control had been broken and the dead placed in the care of the state.

One might ask why it matters whether the church or the state cares for the dead. After all, decedents presumably have no further interest in their remains. Yet in virtually all human societies, the disposition of the dead has been taken very seriously, and degradation of corpses has been viewed as bestial and perverse. Americans were horrified in October 1993, when troops loyal to Somali general Mohamed Aidid dragged the body of a dead U.S. soldier through the streets of Mogadishu.[10]

The preparation of the corpse and the funeral service itself have nearly always been accompanied by rites and ceremonies of various sorts. Some practices seem common to a variety of cultures. For example, the ancient Hebrews, Zarathustrians, Persians, Vedic Indians, and many others emphasized the idea of purifying the body of the decedent in preparation for the funeral ceremony.[11]

In every culture, priests, shamans, and the like have derived much of their influence from their understanding of proper funerary rites that would appease the gods, ease the decedent's way into the next world, and protect the community from the potentially malevolent spirits of the departed. The scribes of ancient Egypt, for example, gained much prestige and influence from their ability to compose scrolls of spells—known collectively today as the *Book of the Dead*—that would be entombed with decedents to enable their souls to navigate the complexities of the afterlife and avoid offending any important deities on their journey to paradise.[12] Wealthy families might purchase lengthy scrolls filled with many useful spells while impecunious decedents would have to make do with one or two spells and trust to luck in their dealings with the gods. It is perhaps no wonder that Thoth was both the Egyptian god of the dead and the god of writing.

Today, it is the state's duty to safeguard remains. And while prayers are sometimes spoken by religious personages, it is the state that claims the power to decide that some may be laid to rest in places of honor, some may be entitled to funerary pomp and ceremony, and some consigned to anonymous potter's fields. What once was a religious matter has become a secular function.

From Parish Register to Coroner's Rolls

In early modern Europe, parish priests were expected to record what today would be called vital statistics, including records of births, baptisms, and burials in their parish registers. These records served both religious and secular purposes and might sometimes be shared with secular authorities to prevent such crimes as bigamy. The typical burial record would include the date of burial, the name and age of the decedent, the decedent's occupation and rank, and their normal place of abode. Some cause of death might also be included though this was not required and often would be recorded simply as "visitation from God," meaning natural causes. The typical birth record would report the date and place of birth and the names of both parents.

Beginning in England in the late twelfth century, and gradually spreading to much of the world, a civil official, the crowner, later called the coroner and later still the medical examiner, took charge of death and burial records, though parish priests often continued to maintain their own registers. The office of the crowner was established under the 1194 Articles of Eyre that mandated three crowners for each county in the realm. More crowners were added over the next several centuries.[13] The term "crowner" derives from the ancient Latin "coronator," an individual who placed a wreath on the head of a decedent, though the term was also taken to indicate that the official was a servant of the crown.

The crowner was assigned a number of official tasks, but the most important of these was the investigation of deaths. The significance of this duty was a function of the complex system of taxes, fees, and fines found in medieval England—a system that functioned to produce substantial revenue for the royal treasury.[14] Quite a variety of rules surrounded the discovery of every death, whether due to disease, accident, or foul play. Whenever a death occurred, witnesses, neighbors, family members, and the community at large were obligated to fulfill numerous requirements. For example, anyone discovering a body was deemed the "first finder" and was obliged to raise the "hue and cry," which meant notifying the four nearest households of the discovery and enlisting them in an impromptu investigation. Any failure by the first finder or the households in question would make them liable to stiff fines. The possibility of such fines often led first finders to drag bodies into neighboring jurisdictions in the hope of transferring the responsibility elsewhere.

After the hue and cry, the local bailiff was required to be summoned and a coroner notified. Failure to promptly send notification to the coroner could mean a substantial fine for the entire community. The community was also responsible for guarding the body until the coroner arrived, which could be several days or even weeks later. Burying or otherwise disturbing the body, even after putrefaction had begun, could produce additional fines, especially so if the coroner's inquest determined that the decedent had been murdered. A homicide would allow the coroner to levy a "murdrum" fine and possibly a "deodand," or forfeiture to the crown of any tool used in the murder. The deodand, the ancestor of today's criminal forfeiture laws, could include something as simple as a knife or as valuable as a horse, carriage, boat, or other object. A murderer's other property and estate were also subject to seizure by the crown.

Through the fines and forfeitures levied by the coroner, death became an important source of revenue for the royal treasury. Since various causes of death and the facts surrounding death had different revenue implications, coroners, who eventually became elected officials, were required to keep records of these matters in the death certificates recorded in their official rolls. Eventually, coroners' rolls became the basis for the official collection of national mortality statistics under the auspices of such statutes as the nineteenth-century English Registration Act. In England's North American colonies, official mortality statistics began to be collected by colonial governments early in the seventeenth century.

In both England and America, early coroners were lay people with no particular medical knowledge. As a result, little credence could be given to officially recorded causes of death. During the nineteenth century, however, England and many U.S. jurisdictions began to require coroners to possess a medical degree, and today the term "medical examiner" has generally replaced the title of coroner. In England, the campaign to require that coroners possess medical credentials was led by Dr. Thomas Wakely, founder of the prominent medical journal *Lancet*, who used his publication to demand that all coroners be physicians. Wakely himself became England's first physician to serve as a coroner.[15]

Efforts to more accurately determine the causes of any particular death were facilitated by the revival of a practice that had been banned by the church—the autopsy—and the evolution of forensic science. Autopsies had been performed since ancient times in the Greco-Roman world and were discussed in some detail in a tenth-century Chinese work titled *The Washing Away of Unjust Imputations*, a detailed text on forensic techniques.[16] In early modern Europe, autopsies were generally prohibited by the church, which forbade the cutting of dead bodies. In the seventeenth and eighteenth centuries, however, European governments even in Catholic countries set aside these clerical restrictions and permitted the use of postmortem examinations where the cause of death or, in the case of homicide, identification of the perpetrator was in doubt. Violence and murder had escalated in the crowded slums of Europe's industrial hubs, and the autopsy became an important tool for the new police and detective bureaus organized in response. Determination of the cause of death became the province of a new medical specialty—pathology. Pathologists and others who studied deaths where foul play was suspected called themselves forensic pathologists or, later, forensic scientists.

Identifying causes of death allowed governments not only to solve crimes but also to assemble mortality data that eventually provided the statistical foundation for public health and safety programs. A major cholera epidemic in nineteenth-century England prompted the enactment of legislation creating a central registration office that compiled all death records and classified them by cause of death. The data compiled by this office convinced the government of the need for the creation of systems of sanitation to prevent the spread of disease.[17] In the United States today, local coroners and medical examiners report deaths to state vital records offices that in turn send their data to the Centers for Disease Control(CDC) National Vital Statistics system. Internationally, the World Health Organization (WHO) endeavors to collect mortality data from every nation to learn and catalogue the causes of the more than fifty million deaths that occur annually around the globe.

Thus, beginning with the office of the coroner and its various equivalents, governments gradually developed the capacity to chart the numbers and causes of deaths within their borders. As we shall see below, possession of these records would eventually allow states to claim that they would, perhaps, conquer death itself by identifying and mitigating each of its causes.

The gradual substitution of official birth certificates for the births recorded in parish records was also important. The church's parish records could be used to establish paternity and legitimacy and so were vital in disputes over property rights. The question of legitimacy was especially important since an illegitimate child could not inherit property. In England, the 1235 Statute of Merton declared, "He is a bastard that is born before the marriage of his parents."[18] The definition also included those who were the products of illicit marriages such as those involving bigamy or incest. This principle was incorporated into the Poor Law of 1576 that barred bastards from inheriting real property and titles even if their parents subsequently wed.[19]

Since parish records were the chief sources of information regarding the dates and circumstances of births and marriages, possession of these records was the foundation of the church's considerable power to rule on matters of marriage, paternity, and legitimacy. The church could, moreover, offer dispensation to important individuals who happened to have been born out of wedlock or wished to have a marriage annulled. These powers were not only important in resolving local disputes but could have far-reaching consequences for the realm. For example, the Catholic Church's assertion that the birth of the future Protestant queen Elizabeth I had been illegitimate led to a great deal of strife including bloody rebellions by groups supporting Elizabeth's Catholic half-sister, Mary.

Beginning in the early 1600s official birth documents began to supplant parish records. The official birth certificate was brief. It generally recorded the date of birth and the names of both parents (if known). Just as the parish record was the foundation of the church's control over matters of family law, the official birth certificate, which rendered parish records superfluous, became a cornerstone of the power of civil law and civil judges in matters of paternity and legitimacy.

Contemporary genetic science and reproductive technology have made questions of parentage both simpler and more complex. On the one hand, DNA largely removes doubt about paternity. On the other hand, thousands of babies are born each year as a result of in vitro fertilization, many using donor eggs and/or donor sperm. Several thousand babies are carried by surrogates, which means that the birth mother has no genetic relationship to the child. Some cases involve surrogates, anonymous egg donors, and anonymous sperm donors, so that neither parent is genetically related to the child. Occasionally, mix-ups in fertility clinics lead to the implantation of eggs in the wrong women and result in women giving birth to one another's babies.[20]

Who are the legal parents? What rights of, say, inheritance do the children possess? These are matters determined by civil law and civil litigation. The state has elbowed aside the church. But even more important, the state has trumped biology in matters of birth. For an example, take the famous case of *Jaycee B. v. Superior Court of California*.[21] Jaycee Buzzanca was born in 1995. John and Luanne Buzzanca had contracted with a surrogate to give birth to the baby and arranged for an IVF procedure involving anonymous egg and sperm donors. In a sense, five persons played a role in Jaycee's conception and gestation. However, just before Jaycee's birth, John filed for divorce and stated that he bore no legal responsibility for the child.

The Orange County Superior Court agreed, saying that Jaycee had no legal parents at all. This decision was reversed by the Fourth District Court of Appeals, which declared that when individuals undertake medical procedures to create a child, a parental relationship is established. This decision is frequently cited and is the basis for the laws of a number of states.[22] Biology might say that the sperm donor, the egg donor, or the gestational mother were the prime candidates for parenthood in Jaycee's case. The courts, however, declared that the Buzzancas, who merely orchestrated the pregnancy, were the parents.

Since time immemorial, humans have employed a basic strategy to transcend their mortality. By identifying with their ancestors and descendants, they have sought to extend the times frames of their lives into the past and future. Long before the advent of the modern-day genealogy industry, veneration of ancestors was a feature of nearly every primitive culture. States have now taken charge of this primordial route to immortality and transformed ancestry and descent from biological facts to political constructs. This clears the way for political concepts like membership in the nation to take precedence over biology. To take an extreme example, even in Nazi Germany, a state built upon and consumed by racial theories, individuals who did not have "Aryan" ancestry could be granted Aryan status for political reasons.[23] Hence, the Japanese were declared to be honorary Aryans as were a number of important military officers who happened to possess Jewish ancestry.[24]

The Hospital

In medieval Europe, monasteries were virtually the only institutional providers of medical care. The sick were generally attended by monks who addressed their afflictions with prayer as well as whatever mundane medical skill they might have. Some orders, such as the Benedictines, did possess considerable medical knowledge based upon their study of ancient medical texts. Like other monastic orders, the Benedictines viewed illness as a divine punishment for sin. They nevertheless studied medical techniques that might amplify the power of prayer. The Saint Gall monastery in Switzerland, for example, was famous for its medical library and the medical training of its monks who used herbal remedies, as well as opiates for the relief of pain, and practiced rudimentary surgical techniques. Many monasteries, like Saint Gall, also functioned as asylums for lepers. Despite the monks' medical learning, prayer and the use of holy relics continued to play a central role at Saint Gall and other monasteries. Medicine and surgery alone were not deemed to be sufficient remedies for disease. Indeed, for the sick, the monasterial hospital was a place of last resort where they could at least be assured of last rites, holy burial, and eternal salvation if they died from their physical affliction.[25]

In the thirteenth and fourteenth centuries, a number of European rulers embarked upon the construction of hospitals to care for the poor and sick. Their design and organization were inspired by the great hospital in Jerusalem constructed by the Knights Hospitaller, a Catholic military order. This hospital, abandoned after the crusaders were expelled from the Holy Land, allowed only trained and experienced physicians to care for patients, applied the principle of triage to give priority to the treatment of the patients whose condition was worst, included a pharmacy to mix drugs, organized patients by type of condition, and emphasized diagnostic methods. Though the Hospitallers were a religious order, secular practices began to assume a priority nearly equal to prayer in the treatment of patients, and their hospital might be seen as a point of transition between the religious hospitals of the past and the secular hospitals of the future.

European hospital construction was prompted initially by an upsurge in disease resulting from wars and religious pilgrimages that brought smallpox and influenza into Europe. This was followed by the acceleration of European urbanization, producing crowded and unsanitary conditions leading to an upsurge of cholera and other diseases. The invention and use of firearms after 1330 led to an enormous increase in severe wounds requiring the services of surgeons as well as the treatment of infections and convalescent care.[26] Later, the arrival of the Black Plague forced the construction of special isolation hospitals, such as the Italian lazarettos, to provide for the quarantine and care of plague victims.

Secular authorities, moreover, saw a healthy populace as a source of state power, particularly when it came to the recruitment of healthy troops for their burgeoning military forces. The church gave its blessing to hospital construction, and religious ceremonies continued to play a role in patient care, but the new hospitals were primarily secular institutions staffed by lay physicians. Indeed, in 1130, the Council of Clermont had declared that monks could no longer practice medicine since this detracted from their religious duties and spiritual goals. This prohibition was never fully enforced but did open the way for nonclergy, including Jews and midwives, to offer medical services to the general populace. Secular authorities were also anxious to prevent their hospitals from coming under clerical control and generally appointed lay administrators to control the hospitals' affairs. Under the new regime, the sick and dying became the concern of the state rather than the church. The overriding purpose of these secular hospitals was to treat and cure disease and to prevent, rather than ease, their patients' passage into the next world.

Philippe Ariès wrote that in modern times the hospital became a place of dying. This may be true in the sense that the hospital replaced the private home as the location of most deaths, but it is a bit misleading, nonetheless. In modern time, individuals are taken to the hospital in an effort to prolong lives that might have been forfeit if they remained in their homes. Some of these individuals die. The medieval hospital was an institution that helped souls on their way to heaven. The modern hospital seeks to delay their journey.[27]

The cemetery, the coroner, and the hospital were three agencies that helped the state replace the church at the border between life and death. From these border outposts, the state began to observe death in all of its manifestations and take a lead role in battling the

Grim Reaper. The first stage in this battle was the introduction and expansion of national public health systems.

From Prayer to Public Health

Though they had precursors in the ancient world, the antecedents of today's national public health programs, at least in Europe, can be traced to the fourteenth century and the crisis of the Black Death that eventually resulted in the death of as much as half of Europe's population. From the perspective of the church, the Black Death was a divine punishment that might be ameliorated by prayer and penitence. Penitence sometimes took the form of self-flagellation. The very devout would whip themselves vigorously for thirty-three consecutive days, one day for each year Jesus was said to have walked the earth.

Since these measures, however dramatic, seemed to have little effect in halting the plague, civil authorities in some regions introduced their own remedies. In 1348, Venice and Florence established public health commissions empowered to prevent the entry of travelers from places known to be infected and to prohibit infected persons from entering public spaces. Other Italian cities followed suit and imposed restrictions on public gatherings in an attempt to halt the plague's spread. The first actual quarantine measures were introduced by the Venetian colony of Ragusa (now Dubrovnik, Croatia) in 1377 and Marseilles in 1383. Travelers seeking to enter these cities were kept in isolation for several weeks before being admitted. During the same period, the Duchy of Milan introduced the ancestor of modern-day monitoring, surveillance, and quarantine systems. The ducal government decreed that all illnesses and deaths in the city must be recorded, and in the case of plague victims, authorities sought to determine the places they had frequented and the persons with whom they might have had close contact. This information could then be used to impose quarantines of potential sources of infection.[28] The gradual disappearance of the Black Death from Europe seemed to confirm the value of these methods, which were adopted throughout Europe over the succeeding centuries.

Over the next two centuries, surveillance became a matter of routine in a number of principalities, especially the Italian city-states, as authorities found that in addition to plague, diseases such as cholera, typhoid, and typhus could be kept in check by monitoring, surveillance, and quarantine.[29] During this period, also, as a precursor to the "sanitation revolution" of the nineteenth century, municipal and, eventually, national governments began to concern themselves with sanitation, including the management of human waste and collection of trash. Both were viewed as possible sources of disease and came under increasingly strict governmental regulation. In England, the 1848 Public Health Act aimed to bring about improvements in municipal sanitation by regulating water supplies, sewers, and drainage under the authority of the General Board of Health.

Through monitoring, surveillance, quarantine, and rudimentary sanitation, government health authorities seemed to conquer the plague, but quite a few other epidemic diseases that afflicted Europe appeared impervious to these measures and would not be brought under control until the advent of mass inoculation and vaccination in the eighteenth century. The most important of these afflictions was smallpox. Smallpox is a severe, highly contagious disease with a case mortality rate of roughly 20 percent. In seventeenth-century Europe the disease killed hundreds of thousands of people each year and worldwide has killed hundreds of millions of people over the past millennium.[30] Smallpox did not respect social class or rank—in the United States both George Washington and Abraham Lincoln contracted smallpox. Lincoln fell ill for a month during the Civil War, soon after delivering his famous Gettysburg Address. News of the president's illness was generally kept from the public.

Methods of preventing smallpox have been in use at least since tenth-century China where the technique of "variolation" was employed. This entailed the inhalation of a powder made from dried smallpox scabs. When the procedure worked, the recipient of the powder developed a mild case of the disease and was henceforward immune. A form of variolation was used in seventeenth-century Europe. This procedure, known as inoculation, consisted of removing a small amount of liquid from an active smallpox pustule and rubbing it into a needle scratch made in the arm of a healthy recipient. When successful, inoculation provided immunity from smallpox though it was a dangerous procedure, requiring a lengthy period of quarantine and convalescence. The procedure's own mortality rate was quite high. When introduced in eighteenth-century England, inoculation was very controversial and denounced by the medical establishment. In the United States, however, important figures like Thomas Jefferson and Benjamin Franklin supported smallpox inoculation. George Washington, for his part, had all his troops inoculated though, again, many became ill.[31]

In the late eighteenth century, Edward Jenner, an English physician practicing in a rural area, famously observed that dairy workers in his region had perfect complexions while most villagers displayed the pockmarks characteristic of smallpox survivors. After looking into this phenomenon Jenner learned that according to local folklore, those exposed to cowpox, a common and generally mild disease then common among cattle, seemed immune to smallpox. Jenner experimented and became convinced that individuals inoculated with cowpox would develop mild symptoms, if any illness at all, and would then be immune to smallpox. The physician had identified a marvelous technique—later to be called vaccination—but found it difficult to persuade decision makers of the importance of his findings.

On the basis of earlier work as a botanist, Jenner was a fellow of the British Royal Society and sought to publish his findings in the *Proceedings of the Royal Society*, England's most prestigious scientific publication. His paper was summarily rejected. Jenner was told that "he was in variance with established knowledge," and that "he had better not promulgate such a wild idea if he valued his reputation." In 1798 Jenner published his work as a pamphlet at his own expense, but in Britain at least, he was initially ridiculed in scientific, political, and even literary circles. Opponents of vaccination declared that the idea of infecting healthy people with diseased matter from animals was outrageous and might even cause vaccinated individuals to sprout horns and take on the appearance of cows.[32]

While Jenner's discovery was still being attacked in England, it found a very sympathetic decision maker across the ocean in the United States. Soon after his election to the presidency in 1800, Thomas Jefferson, an individual quite interested in intellectual innovation and scientific advances, read of Jenner's work when his acquaintance, Harvard professor Benjamin Waterhouse, sent him a copy of Jenner's pamphlet. Subsequently, Waterhouse sent Jefferson more information including some of Jenner's vaccinia and instructions on its preparation, preservation, and administration. Jefferson became extremely enthusiastic about the procedure, strongly encouraged its use in the United States, and even sent a vial of serum along on the Lewis and Clark expedition.[33]

The rapid acceptance and success of smallpox vaccination in the United States, and its support from the nation's political elite, helped to promote the use of Jenner's method in Europe. The advantage of vaccination with cowpox over inoculation with actual smallpox soon became apparent. According to Oldstone, the incidence of death resulting from immunization was reduced from two to three per hundred individuals to one per million persons vaccinated.[34] During the subsequent centuries, large-scale smallpox vaccination—mandatory in England and, at various points in time, in some U.S. municipalities—very nearly eradicated the disease and provided a model for the conquest of other illnesses including polio. Most recently, of course, vaccinations helped to bring the 2020–2021 global covid-19 pandemic under some measure of control. The new public health regime of surveillance, quarantine, sanitation, and vaccination gave the state powerful weapons against death.

Thus, during the late Middle Ages, the churchyard as a burial place, the monasterial hospital, parish death records, and prayer to ward off disease were supplanted by a secular regime that began to place the state squarely in the business of dealing with death. Among the most important, if least heralded, elements of this new thanatotic regime was the collection of mortality statistics that over time, became both a guide and a justification for expansive state action.

The Causes of Death and
The Deconstruction of Mortality

For the medieval coroner, there were essentially four causes of death: murder and manslaughter, accidental death, suicide, and, the most important cause, natural death. Today, the WHO lists more than 350 causes of death including various communicable and noncommunicable diseases, injuries, and violence. What Zygmunt Bauman has called this analytical deconstruction of mortality serves at least two very important functions.[35] First, it creates the impression that dying can be forestalled or, perhaps, even avoided altogether. Death as an abstract concept seems inevitable. Many of these 350 individual causes of death by themselves, however, seem small matters that could be avoided with proper caution, care, and prophylaxis. Fifteen thousand deaths from rabies each year could be avoided by timely vaccination; one hundred thousand maternal deaths each year might not have occurred with proper medical care; eight hundred thousand deaths from hypertension each year might be prevented by medication; sixty thousand deaths each year might be avoided if only individuals learned to shy away from poisonous snakes. Proper precautions might reduce death by violence and by accident. Safer roads and vehicles and more cautious drivers might prevent one million deaths every year.

Examination of the WHO data seems to offer reason for optimism and celebration. Death has always been deemed inevitable, but many if not most of the 350 listed causes of death are preventable or avoidable. Individuals no longer die; they are killed by something that can be resisted, postponed, or avoided altogether.[36] And what of the remaining, still intractable causes of death? Here we come to the second function of the statistical deconstruction of mortality—the opportunity for state action. Governments appear to be working assiduously to mitigate each and every one of these refractory death-dealing agents even as they endeavor to reduce deaths from those already known to be amenable to treatment and prevention.

The United States has been especially active in this domain. The U.S. government's efforts to mitigate death and disease began in 1798 with the creation of the Marine Hospital Service (MHS) to care for sick and injured sailors—a group essential to the health of the new nation's maritime economy. Later, the MHS was charged with conducting medical inspections of individuals entering the United States to prevent diseases from entering the country. In 1912, the MHS was renamed the U.S. Public Health Service and its mission expanded to provide public health services for the nation as a whole. In 1886, the United States established the Hygienic Laboratory to support the MHS's efforts to prevent ships from bringing infectious diseases such as cholera, yellow fever, smallpox, and plague into the United States. The Hygienic Laboratory made use of microbiologist Robert Koch's newly developed methods for isolating bacteria, especially his recent isolation of the bacterium responsible for cholera. The Hygienic Laboratory provided the MHS with a means to scientifically examine passengers and crew members of vessels suspected of harboring disease. In 1930, the Hygienic Laboratory was renamed the National Institute of Health and in 1948, renamed the National Institutes of Health (NIH), began to be subdivided into specialized institutes studying various health problems. The first of these institutes studied dental diseases and heart ailments.

Today, the NIH is an enormous government bureaucracy housed within the Department of Health and Human Services (HHS), boasting an annual budget of more than $43 billion, and consists of twenty-seven institutes and centers, each working to mitigate or cure a specific cause of death. According to the NIH website, one of its major components, the National Cancer Institute, leads an effort to eliminate the suffering and death due to cancer. The National Heart, Lung, and Blood Institute works to prevent and treat diseases related to these organs to help individuals live longer. Other institutes work to fight infectious diseases, alcoholism, diabetes and kidney diseases, and maladies caused by environmental hazards. One institute focuses on the prevention of age-related diseases, surely among the most widespread of the remaining causes of death.

Also housed within HHS are the CDC. The CDC's mission statement declares that the agency's purpose is to save lives by protecting Americans from health threats originating within the nation or abroad. These include infectious diseases, sexually transmitted diseases, and even deaths due to injuries and violence. The CDC was the lead agency in America's battle against COVID-19, though some critics charge that the agency was slow to recognize the threat and to respond to what became a global pandemic.[37]

Americans seem convinced that even more causes of death can be identified and, perhaps, be brought under control by the state. In recent years, advocates concerned with a variety of maladies have sought to define them as public health problems that can have fatal consequences and have demanded that the government take ameliorative action. For example, widespread gun ownership in the United States is said by some to be a leading public health problem and major cause of death—though proponents of gun ownership argue that defensive use of weapons by private owners actually reduces violent deaths.[38] Some have demanded that the government address playground and social-media bullying, which they say is an important cause of suicide by adolescents.[39] Others demand further efforts to end obesity, prevent accidents, and enhance workplace safety. Major federal programs address flood control and the dangers of earthquakes. There is literally no end to the causes of death that call out for mitigation.

As the state endeavors to address the many causes of death, it expands its budget and reach into every corner of society in what may be the ultimate tyranny of good intentions. Schools, homes, business, theaters, arenas, and so forth all come under the jurisdiction of public health rules and different varieties of surveillance from temperature checks and sanitation inspections to vaccination requirements.[40]

In China, currently, prospective travelers must show a green light on their smart phones' public health code apps, showing that they had not been exposed to coronavirus, in order to fly or use other forms of transport. A yellow light indicates possible risk and restricts travel, and a red light indicates exposure, high risk, and a need to quarantine. This system was introduced to curb the spread of COVID-19 and is widely supported as a necessary public health measure. However, the government also uses its control of the app to monitor political dissidents and to prevent them from traveling. "The Chinese government has found the best model for controlling the people," said one Chinese human rights activist whose own health code app had been turned from green to red as he prepared to fly to Shanghai.[41] In the interest of full disclosure, I must say that my own university requires a green light on the school's public health app for access to the campus. Enforcement is lax, but perhaps it is another aspect of the citizenship training colleges claim to provide.

Restrictive public health measures occasionally spark opposition: witness the furor (albeit foolish) in some quarters in both the United States and Europe over mask and vaccination requirements meant to address the COVID-19 epidemic. For the most part, however, state efforts to address the causes of death are popular. Who, indeed, opposes the expansion of research and treatment of heart disease, cancer, and stroke, for example? So, for the most part, the state marches forward, subtly whispering of immortality as it works diligently to mitigate each of the 350 causes of death.

While the NIH and CDC are addressing health problems, other government agencies are working to prevent or at least mitigate various other causes of death. We might include such agencies as the Consumer Product Safety Commission and the Environmental Protection Agency. Indeed, we might say that the chief mission of America's enormous military and police forces is the protection of Americans from violent death.

The fight to disarm the Grim Reaper, however worthwhile, requires a very strong state—in some cases a very intrusive state—that may, in the battle against death, worsen the quality of life. Those who do battle with the Dark Angel, like their priestly forebears, easily become filled with righteous enthusiasm and are reluctant to recognize limits in their work. Consider the example of the ongoing battle against one of the most publicized of the 350 causes of death, terrorism. Terrorism, which on average results in twenty to forty thousand deaths around the world each year, is not among the leading causes of death, but receives considerable media attention and is vigorously fought by a number of nations, including the United States, which for nearly a decade pursued a "global war against terrorism." One aspect of this fight against terrorism has been extensive electronic surveillance both outside and inside U.S. borders to leave the Grim Reaper no place to hide.

Death may be inevitable, but each particular cause of death may be fought and defeated. With the heroic intervention of the state, death becomes contingent, to use Bauman's phrase, rather than certain. In a review of the public health literature, journalist Jacob Sullum noted that contemporary governments "target a wide range of risky habits."[42] These include smoking, drinking, overeating, failing to exercise, owning a gun, and riding a bicycle without a helmet. These risky habits, no doubt, contribute to the WHO's 350 causes of death so should be included in the deconstruction of death we have discussed. Possibly more causes of death remain to be discovered. The WHO's definition of health states, "Health is a state of complete physical, mental, and social well-being and not merely the absence of disease or infirmity."[43] Given this rather broad definition, a full deconstruction of death might include an infinite number of causes and unlimited government action. As Jean Baudrillard observes, decisions about the risk of death are taken from the hands of individuals. "The essential thing is that the decision is withdrawn from them, that their life and their death are never freely theirs, but that they live or die according to a social visa."[44]

Perhaps not surprisingly, many public health initiatives encountered opposition. Generally, opponents questioned the safety and effectiveness of the proposed measures, but often enough, the true source of their resistance was antagonism toward the expansion of state power represented by new public health measures. In the mid-twentieth century, for example, conservative groups in the United States strongly opposed water fluoridation, which they asserted was part of an effort to impose a socialist or communist regime in the

United States.[45] And, since the beginnings of the COVID-19 pandemic, conservative political forces have opposed mandatory vaccination, despite considerable evidence of its effectiveness. Though noisy and troublesome, these groups can generally be seen as fighting a rearguard action. As the state has taken over the borderland between life and death, the Grim Reaper and Big Brother, seemingly adversaries, have become powerful allies.

The Rights of the Dead

M ost of the world's religions postulate some form of after-life. Generally, the faithful and virtuous are promised a reward in the next life while sinners and nonbelievers are threatened with eternal punishment. The boundary between this life and the afterlife, though, can be porous. Many faiths accept the idea that ghosts and other entities from beyond the grave can influence the world of the living. Some pious individuals claim to have glimpsed the next life through such phenomena as near-death experiences, though the validity of these claims is suspect.[1] One best-selling author who wrote about his visit to heaven while in a coma following an auto accident recently admitted to having fabri-cated the entire experience.[2] Since 1840, the Church of Jesus Christ of Latter-Day Saints has practiced the proxy baptism of unbaptized decedents. LDS Church teachings maintain that the souls of the dead can decide whether to accept or reject their baptism.

The secularization of death has at least partially secularized the afterlife. Today the dead, at least the virtuous dead, are promised a secular afterlife built by the state. From this ersatz afterlife the dead can exert posthumous influence by exercising their legal rights—rights that at least figuratively allow decedents to reach back from the grave and influence the world of the living.[3] It may seem peculiar to speak of the rights of decedents. The dead are presumably unaware of any rights that might be granted to them or of any actions that might violate those rights. Yet, under the law, rights generally flow from and are justified by the necessity of protecting legitimate and important individual interests.[4] While the dead may be unaware of their interests, the living often perceive interests in matters that will survive their own deaths or, in some instances, even arise as a result of their deaths. The care of children is an example. Some believe that ensuring the welfare of their descendants gives them a kind of genetic immortality. Hence, it is certainly meaningful to speak of posthumous interests.[5]

The idea of posthumous interests is certainly not novel. Aristotle wrote that good and evil can happen to dead persons. They might receive honors and dishonors and be affected by the good and bad fortunes of their children and other descendants.[6] Similarly, British legal scholar John William Salmond wrote, "There are three things in respect of which the anxieties of living men extend beyond the period of their deaths in such sort that the law will take notice of them. These are a man's body, his reputation and his estate."[7]

In an earlier era, the dead could sue and be sued by the living, and indeed, the dead were sometimes subject to posthumous criminal proceedings. Pope Urban VIII, who had been poisoned, was exhumed and brought to trial for selling church offices. After a guilty verdict, one of the unfortunate corpse's legs was amputated and the remains thrown into the Tiber River. Mundane lawsuits brought against and on behalf of the dead were common in premodern England.[8]

Today, U.S. courts, as well as those in many other nations, recognize the existence of posthumous interests and, accordingly, several categories of posthumous rights. These include testamentary rights, reproductive rights, publicity and reputational rights, privacy rights, and corporeal rights. The dead currently possess some but not all rights guaranteed by the U.S. Constitution.[9] Some posthumous rights, such as testamentary rights, generally come into existence before death and are honored posthumously. Others, such as the right to dignified interment, arise posthumously. The dead, to be sure, do not have the personal ability to enforce their rights, but a machinery does exist for precisely such posthumous enforcement. When it comes to matters of property and reproduction, executors, trustees, and the judiciary will enforce posthumous rights. State attorneys general are charged with making certain that charitable bequests are honored.

Even taken together, these rights might not appear to give the dead the degree of power over the living attributed to fictive zombies and vampires. Yet, through such instruments as wills and estates, their rights do give the dead the ability to direct the use of as much as a trillion dollars in expenditures each year. Compare that to the value of Count Dracula's crumbling castle in Transylvania!

By granting rights to the dead, moreover, the living also address their own fear of death. Humans, observed cultural anthropologist Ernest Becker, are conscious that their own end is inevitable and seek to transcend death through the erection of cultural and institutional legacies that provide the promise of immortality.[10] Our regime of posthumous rights functions as a juridical afterlife that offers the living the hope of an existence after death.

Testamentary Rights

U.S. estate law is based upon the principle of "freedom of disposition." That is, within certain limits, upon their own deaths individuals are free to bequeath their property to whomever they wish and under such terms as they may prescribe. Courts generally will not question the wisdom of the bequest and mainly act to determine the testator's wishes and help give effect to them.[11] Freedom of disposition at death is, however, at least partly circumscribed by estate taxation, spousal entitlements, creditors' rights, the prohibition of racial restrictions, provisions encouraging illegal activity, provisions restraining marriage or promoting divorce, and a small number of other public policy considerations.[12]

The principle of freedom of disposition gives rise, each year, to many cases that seem unfair to the beneficiaries or expectant beneficiaries of a bequest, but the donor's interest almost always outweighs the interests of beneficiaries. In this realm, the dead rule. One frequently cited case that makes the point is *Shapira v. Union National Bank*, decided by the Ohio Court of Common Pleas.[13]

When he died in 1973, David Shapira, MD, left his estate to his three children in equal shares. Dr. Shapira's daughter was married, but his two sons were not, and the will specified that if either son married a non-Jewish woman he would lose his share of the estate. This provision was challenged in Ohio state court by one of the sons, Daniel, who alleged that its enforcement by the court would violate his constitutional rights. In support of his argument, Shapira pointed to the 1967 case of *Loving v. Virginia*, in which the U.S. Supreme Court had called marriage a basic civil right that merited protection from restrictive state action.[14] In the *Loving* case the Supreme Court had struck down a Virginia law banning interracial marriage. Shapira also pointed to the Supreme Court's 1948 decision in the case of *Shelley v. Kramer*.[15] In this case, the court had held that state courts were constitutionally barred from enforcing racially restrictive private real estate covenants. Citing these two precedents, Shapira argued that judicial enforcement of his father's bequest would impose a religious restriction upon his constitutional right to marry a person of his choosing.

The Ohio court, however, rejected Daniel Shapira's claim, saying that the central question at hand was not the son's right to marry but was, rather, the father's right to dispose of his property as he saw fit. The son was always free to marry whomever he pleased. The question was whether he would receive an inheritance and, the court averred, an inheritance was not a right. Accordingly, the court chose to enforce the father's effort to reach from the grave and exert posthumous control over the son's conduct.

Ray D. Madoff cites numerous examples of conditional bequests from recent U.S. cases. One testator required his daughter to "marry a man of true Greek blood and descent and of Orthodox religion" to qualify for her inheritance. Another testator declared his heir was entitled to income from a trust only "so long as she lives up to and observes and follows the teachings and faith of the Roman Catholic church." Another required that his grandchildren remain "members in good standing of the Presbyterian church."[16]

What is often termed "dead hand control" can also be achieved through the use of "incentive trusts." These trusts stipulate that beneficiaries will only receive payments if they meet certain conditions. Examples include the parents of an alcoholic who constructed a trust that after their own deaths, would make payments to their son only if he could prove his sobriety. An Ohio woman, concerned that her son was an unemployed beach bum, made the son's inheritance conditional upon his ability to demonstrate, via regular tax filings, that he was earning an income on his own. One multimillionaire established a trust that made payments to heirs conditional upon their ability to convince an advisory council that "they have attained sufficient wisdom and character" to use the money wisely.[17]

Much of the influence of testators is, indeed, exerted through various forms of trusts. Until recent years, the reach and influence of trusts was limited by the so-called rule against perpetuities that generally restricted an individual's control of property and ability to set conditions on its use to twenty-one years after deaths of those heirs actually living at the time of the trust's creation. After this time, the property was to be free of restrictions on its use by the subsequent heirs. Since the 1950s, though, in order to attract funds to their own financial institutions, most states have eliminated or modified the rule against perpetuities in favor of long-term "dynasty trusts," professionally managed by banks or trust companies. Such trusts may remain valid for decades or even centuries. In Utah and Wyoming, for example, conditions set by testators may at least nominally continue to apply for as long as one thousand years.[18] Generally such trusts are structured in ways that minimize taxation and provide successive generations of heirs with benefits.

Dynasty trusts often include "spendthrift clauses," nominally designed to protect heirs from former spouses, creditors, and their own profligate inclinations. Such clauses generally stipulate that income from the trust is paid to the heirs on some regular basis and cannot be prepaid, attached, or assigned. A dynasty trust filled with conditional bequests conceivably would allow long dead ancestors to influence the religious affiliations, marital plans, and personal conduct of their descendants. As Madoff suggests, this would be the equivalent of enforcing trust provisions today that were created by testators who lived centuries ago.[19]

Charitable Bequests

Testators are also free to make charitable bequests or to establish trusts for charitable purposes. Today, charitable giving of all sorts is seen as a form of beneficence. Until recent years, however, charitable bequests were discouraged by state "mortmain" statutes that disallowed bequests made shortly before the donor's death. These were designed to discourage deathbed bequests to religious organizations and may have, in particular, reflected widespread hostility toward the Catholic Church whose priests were often accused of seeking to persuade dying parishioners to leave their property to the church.[20] Mortmain laws have gradually disappeared, and bequests to charitable entities including those devoted to the promotion of religious values, health care, education, and other public purposes are common provisions of contemporary wills.

Well-to-do individuals often establish charitable trusts or foundations. An ordinary private trust is established for the benefit of one or more individuals. A charitable trust or foundation, by contrast, is established for the furtherance of some charitable purpose. Of course, what constitutes a charity is subject to debate, but courts will generally accept any plausibly good thing—from education and health care to the promotion of excellence in quilting—as a charitable purpose.[21]

Once established, charitable trusts allow donors, called the settlors, to support some charitable endeavor or endeavors long after their own deaths. The principal duties of the trustees of a charitable trust are to implement the intent of the donor, perhaps in perpetuity, even if it might be argued that socially more desirable uses could be found for the money. The donor's intent must be followed as nearly as possible—the legal term is *cy pres*. If, for some reason, the donor's original intent becomes illegal, impossible, or impracticable, a court may allow the trust or foundation to redirect its efforts to some other purpose consistent with the settlors' general charitable goals.[22]

This principle may seem clear and reasonable, but the question of whether the settlor's intentions have been or should be faithfully followed has produced enormous quantities of litigation that generally uphold settlors' rights if they can be determined. An often cited case is that of the Buck Trust. Mrs. Beryl Buck, who died in 1975, left stock eventually worth some $300 million to the San Francisco Foundation. The bequest required the creation of the Leonard and Beryl Buck Foundation to be used exclusively for charitable purposes in Marin County, California.

Marin County is one of the wealthiest areas in the United States, and the San Francisco Foundation petitioned the state court for cy pres to allow it to divert some of the income from the estate to less affluent areas surrounding Marin County. This effort was opposed by Marin County officials who called the foundation's trustees "grave-robbing bastards."[23] After a six-month-long legal battle, the court dismissed the foundation's cy pres petition and ordered the creation of a Marin County Foundation that would administer the Buck Trust in accord with the wishes of the settlor.

Testamentary rights, to be sure, are not absolute. Courts may set aside provisions that are impossible to carry out or run counter to public policy. In 1981, for example, a number of groups objected to a $30,000 bequest from journalist Fred Sparks to the Palestine Liberation Organization (PLO). The objectors charged that the PLO was a terrorist organization and should, as a matter of public policy, be barred from receiving the bequest. The New York courts were sympathetic to the objection and insisted that the terms of the bequest be altered to direct the money to more peaceful Palestinian groups.[24] In a similar vein, in the 1966 case of *Evans v. Newton*, the U.S. Supreme Court held that the late Senator Augustus Bacon's bequest of land to the city of Macon, Georgia, via a trust that would maintain a park restricted to the use of white people was unconstitutional, and the settlor's intent could not be followed.[25] In the subsequent case of *Evans v. Abney*, however, the court gave the settlor a partial victory when it ruled that a plan to modify the bequest to racially integrate the park would be inconsistent with Bacon's wishes. Hence, the trust was dissolved and the funds reverted to Bacon's heirs.[26]

Though not absolute, testamentary rights are afforded substantial judicial deference. Indeed, in quite a number of cases, federal courts have indicated that government interference with an owner's right to dispose of property in a will or trust can be understood as a "taking" prohibited by the Constitution's Fifth Amendment—even though in some instances the property owner has long been dead.[27] Thus, in the 1979 case of *Midkiff v. Tom*, the U.S. District Court of Hawaii heard a challenge from the trustees of the estate of Princess Bernice Pauahi Bishop, who had been deceased for more than a century, to the state's use of eminent domain to seize the land held by the estate and sell it in building lots.[28] The district court ruled in favor of the estate and its judgement was affirmed by the Ninth Circuit Court of Appeals, though eventually the U.S. Supreme Court ruled against the estate and allowed the taking. Despite this outcome, what is important here is that three federal courts, including the U.S. Supreme Court, accepted the idea that the testamentary rights of a long dead landowner deserved constitutional protection. This point was underscored by the U.S. Supreme Court in the 1987 case of *Hodel v. Irving*.[29] Here, the court held that the owner's right to hand on property at death is a significant aspect of property ownership and is, therefore, protected by the Fifth Amendment. The court declared, indeed, that the right to pass on property to one's heirs had been a part of the Anglo-American legal tradition since feudal times.

Wills and estates are often contested, usually by disgruntled family members who believe that they have been treated unfairly. Typically, unhappy would-be heirs assert that the testator lacked mental capacity or was unduly influenced by some other individual in drafting the will. Such challenges seldom succeed.[30] Wills are assertions of property rights, and in death as in life persons are generally free to dispose of their property as they see fit, even if they do so in ways that seem foolish or unfair to others.

Reproductive Rights

At first blush, the idea that deceased individuals have the right to reproduce—or not—might seem a bit far-fetched. After all, how can a decedent reproduce? Medical science, however, has created postmortem reproductive possibilities such as those involving frozen sperm and ova and fetuses developing within brain-dead women. As Smolensky observes, these medical possibilities have given rise to posthumous reproduction cases, mainly involving the use of frozen gametes, in which the rights of decedents figure prominently.[31]

Where the posthumous disposition of frozen gametes is at issue, so long as the intent of the decedent is clear, courts have generally given precedence to the decedent's wishes over those of others claiming an interest in the matter. Take, for example, the case of *Hecht v. Superior Court*.[32] This case arose because, in his will, William Kane had bequeathed to his girlfriend, Deborah Hecht, fifteen vials of sperm that he had cryobanked for her future insemination. After Kane's death by suicide, his two adult children from a previous marriage challenged this provision of the will. The children argued that the sperm should be destroyed or, alternatively, following the terms of the estate's property settlement that awarded Hecht 20 percent of Kane's property, that she was entitled to only three vials of the frozen sperm. Presumably, Kane's children had an interest in reducing the probability that Hecht would become pregnant and, failing that, limiting the number of Kane's posthumous children that might be conceived.

The probate court ruled against Hecht and actually ordered the destruction of the sperm, but the Superior Court of Los Angeles County reversed the probate court and awarded Hecht all fifteen vials of sperm. For the court, the decisive point was Kane's clearly expressed intent: "the will evidences the decedent's intent that Hecht, should she so desire, is to receive his sperm stored in the sperm bank to bear his child posthumously."

The decedent's intent also played a central role in the case of *Woodward v. Commissioner of Social Security*.[33] In the *Woodward* case, a husband and wife banked the husband's sperm after he was diagnosed with leukemia. Two years after the husband's death, his wife was inseminated with the banked sperm and gave birth to twins. The Massachusetts Supreme Judicial Court found that the children were entitled to receive their late father's Social Security benefits. The court ruled that posthumously conceived children were entitled to benefits from a parent's estate so long as the decedent had "clearly and unequivocally" consented to such posthumous reproduction.

Privacy Rights

In rulings regarding posthumous privacy rights, U.S. courts historically have been concerned with the privacy rights of survivors rather than decedents though, increasingly, courts have found that the posthumous right of privacy also arises from decedents' own interest in preserving their "dignity." The leading privacy case is the U.S. Supreme Court's ruling in the case of *National Archives and Records Administration v. Favish*.[34] The case arose from charges that the 1993 death of deputy White House counsel Vincent Foster had been a homicide disguised as a suicide. Various conspiracy theories were reported by the media linking, among others, President Bill Clinton to Foster's death. Attorney Allan Favish was a well-known proponent of such theories and filed suit under the Freedom of Information Act demanding that the National Archives be compelled to release crime scene and autopsy photographs he claimed might prove that Foster had been murdered.

Favish prevailed in U.S. district and appellate courts in California that agreed that there was a compelling public interest in disclosing what Favish said could be evidence of a government cover-up. The

U.S. Supreme Court, however, overturned these decisions and ruled, instead, in favor of privacy interests. Justice Anthony Kennedy writing for a unanimous court said, "Family members have a personal stake in honoring and mourning their dead and objecting to unwarranted public exploitation that, by intruding upon their own grief, tends to degrade the rights and respect they seek to accord to the deceased person who was once their own." The court rejected Favish's demand that the photos be made public. The court was, however, careful to point out that the right to privacy belonged to the living, not the dead. The court cited an 1895 New York Court of Appeals decision on this point. "It is the right of the living not of the dead which is recognized . . . to protect their feelings and to prevent a violation of their own rights in the character and memory of the deceased."[35]

Subsequent court decisions followed the *Favish* precedent in recognizing that the families had a right to be protected from the public disclosure of photographs, last words, and other information pertaining to their deceased relatives. Hence, a Rhode Island court blocked media access to tapes of the 911 calls made, just before their deaths, by victims of a 2003 fire that killed ninety-six persons in a Warwick, Rhode Island, night club. Similarly, in 2005, the *New York Times* was blocked from obtaining tapes of the dying words uttered by 911 callers from the World Trade Center to emergency operators before the buildings collapsed. The newspaper asserted that readers had a right to know if the 911 system had performed adequately. New York's highest court, however, ruled that relatives' privacy interests outweighed the public's interest in the matter.[36]

In these and many other cases, courts pointed to the privacy interests of family members as reasons for refusing to allow public access to decedents' images. In a growing number of cases, however, courts have recognized that decedents may have their own privacy interests. This recognition revolves around the idea that the dead are entitled to be treated with dignity so that when family members or others seek to prevent the publication of photographs, dying words, medical and autopsy records, and so forth, they are acting on behalf of the deceased as well as protecting their own interests.

Thus, for example, when it ruled against the effort by the *New York Times* to obtain the dying words of those killed in the 9/11 terror attack, the New York Court of Appeals said, "The desire to preserve the dignity of human existence even when life has passed is the sort of interest to which legal protection is given under the name of privacy."[37] Similarly, the Superior Court of Rhode Island pointed to the "desirability of preserving individual dignity" in ruling that the media were not entitled to publicize Rhode Island fire victims' dying words. In another pertinent case, the Supreme Court of Washington held that "the immediate relatives of a decedent have a protectable privacy interest in the autopsy records of the decedent. That protectable privacy interest is grounded in maintaining the dignity of the deceased."[38]

"Dignity-of-death" jurisprudence seems to be gaining increased recognition in U.S. law.[39] This idea of death with dignity seems to underlie physician-assisted suicide legislation such as Oregon's Death With Dignity Act and similarly named statues enacted in Maine, Washington, and the District of Columbia. And, though new to U.S. law, the idea that decedents have a right to dignity is commonly accepted in western Europe. Madoff discusses an Italian case in which an individual named Franco Scoglio died during the filming of a television program. Italy's Authority for the Protection of Privacy decreed that images of Scoglio's death could not be displayed because it would be a violation of the decedent's right to privacy.[40] Similarly, when an Italian magazine obtained photos of Princess Diana's dead body taken when emergency personnel arrived at the scene of the fatal accident as well as the subsequent autopsy report, an Italian court ruled that the pictures and report could not be published because that would violate Diana's personal dignity.

In a German case the constitutional court prohibited the publication of a novel in which one of the characters was based upon the life of the late actor and theater director Gustav Grundgens, who was alleged to have cooperated with the Nazis to advance his career. Grundgens's family denied this allegation and brought suit to halt the novel's publication. The court said an individual's death did not end the obligation of the law to protect his dignity.[41]

U.S. law does not offer decedents the same general privacy rights guaranteed by European laws. One realm, however, in which the privacy rights of decedents is specifically recognized in the United States is the privacy of health information. Most states restrict access to death certificates listing the cause of death and contributing health factors. And, under the terms of the federal HIPAA Privacy Rule published in 2013, individually identifiable health insurance information about a decedent is protected for fifty years following the death of the individual. This rule is designed to protect the privacy of decedents, not family members. Indeed, individuals may bar family members from posthumous access to their health records.[42]

Defamation

Chilon of Sparta, according to legend, one of the sixth-century Seven Sages of Greece, was reputed to have been the first to advise against speaking ill of the dead—a maxim that is frequently repeated, though often disregarded. Can the dead be harmed by those who speak ill of them? The answer is no and yes. On the one hand, the dead are beyond being harmed by the opinions of the living. On the other hand, the living can certainly have an interest in what others will say about them after their deaths. Don Herzog offers a hypothetical example. Imagine that a community leader dies while leading an effort to renovate the city's parks. After his death someone spreads a rumor that the decedent was an embezzler and a child molester. "Who wants to keep working on what's mordantly dubbed the Child Molester Park Project?" Herzog asks.[43] Thus, living individuals who have an interest in the completion of projects or the value of property they plan to bequeath to family members have a stake in avoiding posthumous attacks upon their reputations.

Posthumous charges of child molestation levied against British media personality Jimmy Savile forced the closure of two charities that had been identified with Savile, the Jimmy Savile Charitable Trust and the Jimmy Savile Stoke Mandeville Hospital Trust. In the United States, posthumous charges of child molestation made against Michael Jackson led to calls for boycotts of the late singer's work and a sharp drop in the value of his estate.

It is not only the material interests of children and other descendants that can be harmed by the reputations of long-dead ancestors. Family members and descendants can suffer psychological and social harm from the shame associated with the deeds of the dead. As the biblical book of Proverbs declares (10:7), "The memory of the righteous is a blessing, but the name of the wicked will rot."

For example, descendants of Dr. Samuel A. Mudd, a physician who treated John Wilkes Booth after he shot President Abraham Lincoln, have been fighting for nearly 150 years to clear the family name. Dr. Mudd was convicted of aiding and abetting the assassins, but his descendants say he did not know Booth and did not know of the assassination until after Booth and his accomplice departed. Many of Mudd's descendants say his conviction has "a continuing impact on the Mudd family." They claim that Mudd's son became an alcoholic because of the shame and that members of subsequent generations constantly feared revelations of the family's "dark secret." Even the phrase "your name is mud" gained currency after the assassination.[44] Similarly, the children of Julius and Ethel Rosenberg fought for years to clear their parents' names. The Rosenbergs had been convicted and executed in 1953 as spies for the Soviet Union. When they reached adulthood, the sons were determined to prove their parents' innocence and posthumously restore their good names. Unfortunately, their lengthy efforts failed, and after sifting through mountains of evidence they themselves became convinced that their parents had been guilty.

Despite the potential material, social, and psychological costs of posthumous reputational damage, neither U.S. courts nor U.S. (or British) law has been much concerned with the matter. Smith observes that courts in both nations have generally rejected the notion of civil liability for defaming the dead.[45] Six American states do, however, have statutes that criminalize defamation of the dead. Kansas law prohibits communications that "degrade and vilify the memory of one who is dead," while Oklahoma prohibits the malicious communication of material "designed to blacken or vilify the memory of one who is dead."[46] Such laws are seldom enforced and tend to be viewed skeptically by the courts.

Of course, the possibility of posthumous defamation has implications for the memory or dignity of the deceased. As we saw in the case of privacy rights, these intangibles are more important in some nations than in the United States, which tends to be more concerned with property interests. Chinese courts, for example, have accepted the importance of protecting decedents' reputations from posthumous slanders. The case of "Hehua Girl," decided in 1989 by the Supreme Peoples' Court, is considered a landmark in this realm of Chinese law.[47] Hehua Girl was the stage name of a well-known actress, Ji Wenzhen, who died in 1944 at the age of nineteen. Many years later a newspaper published, in a series of articles, a novel that purported to be an account of Ji's brief life. The novel included many sensational, albeit unverified, assertions, including graphic illustrations, of the actress's alleged sexual promiscuity.

Ji Wenzhen's mother sued the newspaper for defamation. In its eventual decision, the court recognized the concept of a "posthumous reputational right" that could be vindicated by a decedent's relatives. The court banned publication of the book and ordered the defendant to make a public apology and pay restitution. In a series of subsequent decisions, the same court affirmed the idea that the "reputation of the dead" merited judicial protection.

Posthumous Publicity Rights

Like privacy rights, publicity rights refer to the control of information. But, while privacy rights are designed mainly to protect intangible commodities, individual dignity and reputation, publicity rights are concerned mainly with the economic value of information about individuals. Living persons, particularly famous or notorious individuals, can benefit from the sale of numerous forms of intellectual property including likenesses, interviews, autographs, and mementos of various sorts. Such publicity rights can be quite lucrative and are protected by law. And, just as the courts and legislation have given individuals the right to posthumously dispose of other sorts of property, it is not surprising that posthumous publicity rights are recognized by the laws and courts of many U.S. states. The value of posthumous property rights is enormous. The marketing, licensing, and commercial use of deceased celebrities is an estimated $3 billion business. Among the top posthumous earners was Michael Jackson. In just the first year after his death in 2009, Michael Jackson's estate earned more than $1 billion by licensing his name, likeness, and music.[48] After his reputation was posthumously damaged by claims of child molestation, the value of Jackson memorabilia dropped sharply.

No celebrity, not even Michael Jackson, can profit posthumously from their own fame. Those who possess publicity rights, however, like individuals who own any sort of valuable property, have an interest in disposing of those rights to persons or organizations of their own choosing—perhaps even selling them in advance of their own deaths. Presumably this is why Hollywood celebrities applauded then governor Arnold Schwarzenegger's campaign on behalf of legislation that amended California's publicity rights statute to provide for testamentary rights. This California statute, popularly known as the "Dead Celebrities Bill," was signed by Schwarzenegger in 2007 and recognized a posthumous right of publicity, "freely transferable or descendible in whole or in part by contractor by means of any trust or any other testamentary interest."[49]

In principle, a posthumous right of publicity might have no termination date, but on average, the states that grant such a right allow it a duration of fifty years. The great exception is Tennessee, which allows the right of publicity to continue indefinitely. Since Tennessee is the former home of Elvis Presley, his estate can continue to reap the benefits of Elvis's fame as long as he is remembered.[50] This result might seem to belie the title of Presley's famous song "Its Now or Never," which might more correctly have been titled "Its Now and Forever."

Copyright

Also contributing to the growing influence of the dead is the ever-expanding scope and duration of copyright protection in the United States. A copyright gives its owner the exclusive right to produce copies of a creative work, such as a book, film, or musical composition, for some specified period of time. Others are prohibited from making such copies except with the permission of the copyright holder, who may require the payment of a fee as a condition for permission.

The first copyright law was enacted in England in 1709, giving publishers rights to printed works for a fixed period. In the United States, the Constitution authorizes the government to enact copyright legislation, "to promote the progress of science and useful arts, by securing for limited times for authors and inventors, the exclusive right to their respective writings and discoveries." Such legislation currently fills volumes in the U.S. Code. To administer federal copyright law Congress, in 1790, established the U.S. Copyright Office, which registers copyright claims and records information about copyright ownership.

Originally, copyright protection in the United States applied mainly to books; those seeking a copyright were required to take action to register their claim; the copyright applied only to an exact copy of the work in question; and copyrights were of limited duration.[51] America's first copyright law offered protection for only fourteen years and allowed renewal of the copyright for another period of fourteen years if the copyright holder was still living. The presumption was that a copyright was intended to protect the living and would lapse with the death of the material's creator.

Today, copyright can apply to almost any form in which ideas can be expressed—poems, films, dance routines, and so forth. In principle ideas themselves cannot be protected by copyright; only the form in which they are expressed can be copyrighted. However, copies need not be precise but merely derived from the original work. A film, for example, may violate a book's copyright.

In this way, once copyrighted in one form, ideas are effectively copyrighted.

Most important for our present purposes, the duration of the validity of copyrights has increased over the years. Under current federal law, the duration of a copyright is the life of the author plus seventy years. Thus, copyrights can outlive the creators.

Copyrights give their holders considerable power over the use of their creations, and copyrights are a form of property that can be sold or bequeathed to others. Generally speaking, however, the rights of copyright creators—living or dead—are sharply reduced when the ownership of a copyright changes hands. In the event of a conflict, courts will generally defer to the rights of copyright holders over those of creators. Once a copyright has been transferred, the creator generally retains no residual rights, and copyright holders may use the work or block its use in ways that might not be consistent with the intent of the creator. For example, James Joyce's grandson, who holds the copyright to Joyce's work, has attached stringent and often idiosyncratic limits upon its performance or publication. Joyce himself enjoyed his fame and was eager to have his work read, performed, and sung. In some cases, copyright holders may find it expedient to voluntarily surrender their rights. For example, the authors of an academic work may prefer to surrender the copyright to the publisher so that the latter will deal with requests for reprints and permissions. More frequently, a copyright holder will, for a fee, license the right to use a work rather than transfer the copyright.

Moral Rights

In recent years, copyright has been joined by another form of protection for the rights of artists and authors. This is the idea of moral rights, a legal concept that has played an important role in Europe for several decades and gained a foothold in the United States in 1998 when Congress enacted the Visual Artists Rights Act (VARA) to conform to U.S. obligations under the Berne Convention that, among other things, requires signatory states to protect artists' moral rights.

Moral rights include the right of paternity and right of integrity.[52] Paternity means that artists and authors have a continuing right to have their names associated with their work; integrity means that the original artist possesses residual rights in the work and may continue to control its use even after the copyright is sold. Integrity also means that the work or performance may not be treated in a derogatory manner, resulting in its destruction or mutilation, or in a manner prejudicial to the author's honor or reputation. When Congress enacted VARA, it limited the law's coverage to paintings and similar art forms and did not provide artists with posthumous rights. In countries where moral rights are well established, though, they apply to books, films, paintings, and other art forms that endure after the artist or author's death—usually for a period of seventy years. In France, the moral right of integrity is perpetual.

Where artists and authors do have posthumous rights, it is generally up to their descendants to bring suit when they believe those rights to have been violated. Often, the question to be decided by a court is whether some contemporary effort to make use of the work in question offends the honor or diminishes the reputation of the artist by using the work in a manner inconsistent with the artist's intent. In France, courts have asserted that the postmortem use of work that is likely to diminish respect for its creator is forbidden.[53]

Where an author or artist has left clear instructions about the meaning of the work and a clear prescription for its use, European courts will generally defer to the deceased author's wishes. Of course, most cases do not offer clear instructions and require courts to make their own determinations. In a famous French case, Victor Hugo's great-great-grandson Pierre Hugo alleged that a publisher who brought out and marketed two books as nominal sequels to Hugo's 1862 classic *Les Misérables* had violated Hugo's moral right of integrity by changing the story and altering several major characters. This case was heard by three French courts over a period of several years.

The publisher asserted that Victor Hugo had specifically endorsed the idea that his work would be used and modified by succeeding generations after his death. The publisher relied on, among other documents, an 1878 speech in which Hugo said, "Before publication, the author undoubtedly has unlimited rights. . . . But as soon as the work is published the author no longer has absolute control over it. At that point, another character takes control . . . human spirit, public domain, society. . . . Once the author is dead . . . I would choose . . . the rights of the public domain." For his part, Pierre Hugo cited Victor Hugo's statement that "once the book is published, once the sex of the book, whether masculine or not, has been identified and proclaimed, once the child has cried his first cry, the book should be left to live or die as it is." After years of litigation, the French courts concluded that Victor Hugo's wishes could not be decisively determined.[54]

Despite the outcome of the Hugo case, deceased authors and artists can exercise far more influence through moral rights than via copyright protection. In the United States, film director John Huston, for example, was not able to prevent the Turner Entertainment Co., which held the copyright, from colorizing several of his films for television broadcast. Huston thought colorization destroyed the artistic integrity of a film and compared it to pouring sugar water on a roast. Under U.S. copyright law, though, Huston possessed no residual rights to his films, so was powerless to prevent Turner's colorization project. In France, however, after Huston's death, his estate was able to prevent the broadcast of colorized versions of Huston's films. The court said that black and white was Huston's aesthetic choice and that colorization violated the deceased director's moral rights. The fact that, during his life, Huston had publicly opposed colorization of his films was central to the court's decision.[55]

The concept of posthumous moral rights is gradually gaining traction in the United States. U.S. courts have increasingly become willing to consider whether to hear posthumous moral rights cases brought under foreign law.[56] The idea of posthumous moral rights, moreover, has gained a measure of legitimacy in public discussions of artistic issues. Thus, for example, when a manufacturer made use of a take-off of a Beastie Boys song in one of its commercials, it quickly agreed to stop when informed that a deceased member of the group had opposed the use of his music in advertising. In an open letter, the manufacturer stated, "we were completely unaware that the late, great, Adam Yaunch had requested in his will that the Beastie Boys songs never be used in advertising. . . . We would like to respect his wishes.[57] Why was the company so anxious to respect the Beastie Boys' moral rights? The answer is simple. Today, many customers, especially younger persons, want to do business only with companies that take appropriate moral and political positions. In essence, by respecting the posthumous moral rights and reputation of the deceased, Adam Yaunch, the manufacturer hoped to bolster its own reputation. The admonition to never speak ill of the dead has simply taken on new forms.

Corporeal Rights

A final set of rights possessed by the dead concerns the treatment of their remains—their bodies and body parts. Presumably the dead no longer care about their bodies, but the living often have feelings about how their bodies will be treated after death. Most people, albeit not all, prefer that their remains be treated in a dignified manner. In this hope, they are usually joined by children, friends, and relatives who may be prepared to see to it that their loved ones' remains are treated respectfully. Most individuals view mistreatment of a corpse as the ultimate form of degradation, while respect for a corpse is an affirmation of the decedent's humanity.[58]

In the United States, the criminal laws of most states prohibit the abandonment, concealment, or abuse of dead bodies. And, at least since the early nineteenth century, state courts have done their part to protect the dignity of the dead. One early and often cited case is *In re Kanavan* decided by Maine's Supreme Court in 1821.[59] The question at hand was whether a defendant could be criminally charged for throwing the body of a dead infant into a river. The court held that it was a crime to deny a person a decent burial or to dispose of a body without a funeral. A century later, the same court held that it was a criminal offense to dispose of a body in a manner contrary to common decency.[60] Until recent years, neither state statutes nor court decisions were concerned with aborted fetuses. Under pressure from the antiabortion movement, however, most states have developed rules requiring the "dignified" disposal of the remains, particularly if the fetus has reached a stage of development that includes cartilaginous structures or skeletal parts.

Often, decedents leave instructions regarding their funerals and the disposition of their bodies. Whether or not these instructions are followed is generally up to the family members or friends who make the actual funeral arrangements. One famous decedent whose instructions were not fully followed was the English Utilitarian philosopher Jeremy Bentham, who asked that his body be preserved so that it could be wheeled out at parties if his friends missed him. The body was preserved and put on display at University College, London (UCL). Unfortunately, his head was not properly preserved so was not displayed with the body. At one point the head was stolen by students from UCL's rival, King's College. The head was eventually recovered, and both the body and head are on display at UCL but seldom attend parties.

Many other individuals seem less concerned with their heads than their headstones and, in their wills, stipulate particular inscriptions. Consider the following final thoughts:

Comedian Rodney Dangerfield: "There Goes the Neighborhood."
Singer Dean Martin: "Everybody Loves Somebody Sometime" (a verse from a song Martin made famous).
Comedian Jackie Gleason: "And Away We Go" (Gleason's iconic show opener).
Talk show host Merv Griffin: "I Will Not Be Right Back After This Message" (Griffin was tired of commercial interruptions).
Screenwriter Billy Wilder: "I'm a Writer, But Then Nobody's Perfect."

Singer and actor Frank Sinatra: stipulated that he be buried with a pack of Camel cigarettes, a bottle of Jack Daniels whiskey, and the inscription, "The Best is Yet to Come" (a hopeful refrain from one of Sinatra's best known songs). William Shakespeare, concerned that grave robbers would disturb his rest, had his headstone inscribed with an entreaty and a threat:

> Good friend, for Jesus' sake forbeare,
> To dig the dust enclosed here.
> Blessed be the man that spares these stones,
> And cursed be he that moves my bones."

Some individuals leave somewhat odd funeral instructions. For example, writer Hunter S. Thompson stipulated in his will that his body be cremated and his ashes shot from a cannon. At his 2005 funeral, not only were Thompson's ashes shot from the cannon, but some were mixed into the fireworks detonated over the grave site. Reportedly, the entire event was bankrolled by actor Johnny Depp, who had portrayed Thompson in the 1998 film *Fear and Loathing in Las Vegas*.[61]

Instructions regarding inscriptions and other funeral directions, even if stated clearly in a decedent's will, are generally not considered binding upon descendants and trustees and are often disregarded. Thus, for example, baseball legend Ted Williams explicitly stated in his will that his remains were to be cremated and the ashes thrown into the sea off the Florida coast. This stated intent did not comport with the wishes of some family members, who had Williams's body and head separately placed in cryonic suspension in vats of liquid nitrogen in the hope that a cure for the form of leukemia that killed Williams might be found in the future and the baseball star thawed and brought back to life.[62]

Individuals cannot exercise control over the dispositions of their remains because, in the United States, persons do not have a property interest in their remains. They may, as we saw earlier, bequeath property to whomever they wish and attach conditions and stipulations to the bequest. However, no person can bequeath his or her body to another. They may request that the body be burned and shot from a cannon or given to a medical school to help train future doctors, but these requests are not binding upon the administrators of decedent's estates. The same lack of a property interest in the body also means that the proper government agency can perform an autopsy, regardless or any prior wishes stated by the decedent, if that agency deems a postmortem examination necessary for reasons of public health or safety.

While individuals may not control what happens to their remains, every U.S. state has enacted laws governing the disposition of corpses. Such statutes are, in part, designed to protect the public health and the interests of family members, but they are also intended to protect the right of the dead to be treated with dignity. The *Kanavan* court declared that proper burial was required by good morals, decency, and the "reverential respect" owed to sepulchers. The Utah Supreme Court said a proper funeral was required by the "dictates of humanity."[63] Similarly, the criminal laws of most states protect the dead against "undignified disturbance" after their interment. The laws of every state prohibit the desecration of tombs and require a court order before a corpse can be disinterred. Of course, in the fullness of time, every cemetery fills and many suffer bankruptcy. Usually state and county governments may eventually "repurpose" the land, forcing relocation of the graves to allow the construction of homes, highways, and golf courses on the old burial sites.

Body parts present special problems. Most states encourage the donation of organs for transplantation, and many have enacted "presumed consent" statutes that allow medical examiners to donate transplantable body parts from any corpse whose death is being investigated. The presumed consent rule can lead to controversies between medical examiners' offices and families that discover that organs have been taken from a deceased relative without their knowledge or consent.

The medical use of a decedent's discarded tissues or cells can also become controversial. In a frequently cited case, the Supreme Court of California has ruled that such materials are not the (dead or living) person's property and can be used for medical or commercial purposes.[64] This idea, however, came under sharp attack in 2013 when the family of Henrietta Lacks learned that Johns Hopkins University had commercialized cancerous cells taken from Ms. Lacks's body at autopsy in 1951. What came to be called the HeLa cell line had characteristics that made it valuable to many different sorts of researchers and scientists throughout the world and has generated hundreds of millions of dollars in royalties and profits for commercial users of the cells, though Johns Hopkins says it never patented Lacks's cells and never profited from their use. In 2013, some members of the Lacks family agreed on a settlement brokered by the National Institutes of Health that gives Lacks recognition for her contribution and allows the family a voice in the use of the cells but no financial reward. Other members of the Lacks family have filed suit against Johns Hopkins.

Another controversy involving the medical use of material taken from decedents is the area of fetal tissue research. Fetal tissue plays a major role in biomedical science, but almost all this research involves the use of tissue from elective abortions. Antiabortion groups oppose the use of such fetal tissue, and during the Trump era severe restrictions were placed on the medical use of fetal tissue. These restrictions were dropped by the Biden administration. Donald Trump's detractors liked to point out that two drugs administered to the former president when he was hospitalized for COVID-19 in 2020 were developed using research on fetal tissue.[65] Perhaps the president was unaware of the provenance of casirivimab/imdevimab and remdesivir when he touted their efficacy after his recovery.

Rights of the Dying

Like the corporeal rights of the dead, the rights of the dying affirm the idea that death—or in this case the approach of death—should not rob individuals of their dignity. Thus, the dying must be treated with respect. But beyond simple respect, in the modern world the dying are often accorded the right to make choices about their deaths.[66] The most important realm in which the rights of the dying come into play is that of individuals' wishes regarding end-of-life medical care. Thousands of Americans are kept alive for long periods of time by aggressive medical intervention including feeding tubes, dialysis, and artificial ventilation. As many as thirty thousand are permanently comatose or survive for months or years in vegetative states.[67] To some extent, this is the result of advance medical directives signed by individuals who indicate they want all possible life-sustaining treatments to be used. In other instances, family members make the decision.

In the early twentieth century, Justice Benjamin N. Cardozo declared that all persons had the right to determine what medical procedures might be performed on them and to refuse consent to procedures they did not want.[68] Cardozo's comments are seen as providing the basis for the idea that individuals are entitled to consent, or not, to medical procedures.[69] In recent years, the Supreme Court has affirmed this idea. In the important 1990 case of *Cruzon by Cruzon v. Director Missouri Department of Public Health*, the court declared that constitutional due process protected both an interest in life and an interest in refusing life-sustaining medical equipment.[70]

Federal law and the laws of most states allow individuals to specify the level of life-prolonging medical intervention they prefer if they suffer from an incurable condition. At the federal level, the Patient Self-Determination Act (PDSA) requires healthcare facilities that receive Medicare or Medicaid funding to provide patients with information on their "end of life" options. Facilities are required to tell patients that they may accept or refuse medical services and determine whether patients have executed advance medical directives. Since the enactment of PDSA the number of patients who provide hospitals and nursing homes with advance directives has increased sharply. Typically, an advance directive indicates whether or not the individual wishes to allow cardiopulmonary resuscitation, is willing to be placed on a ventilator, is willing to be fed through a tube, is willing to accept blood transfusions, will allow dialysis or life-prolonging surgery or antibiotic therapy, and is or is not willing to accept maximum pain relief even if this might accidentally hasten their death. The individual may also name an advocate or agent to make these decisions for them.

While the PDSA and increased patient use of advance directives might appear to provide dying individuals with a good deal of control over their end-of-life treatment, the reality is more complicated. To begin with, it is not clear whether an individual's decision made when he or she might still be healthy will accurately represent their preferences when they are actually deathly ill. A dying person might have a different attitude toward eschewing aggressive medical intervention than a person for whom this is merely a hypothetical question.[71] Often enough, too, hospitals are not able to find advance medical directives (though registries exist for these directives) when they are needed, and in the absence of a clear and fully executed directive, a patients' family members' insistence on aggressive treatment will often be followed by the medical staff. Under such circumstances, physicians and hospitals incur more legal risk from failing to undertake aggressive treatment than from so doing. Another reason that patients' advance directives may be ignored is the existence of emergency conditions that force hospitals and physicians to allocate scare resources to those most likely to benefit from treatment, possibly refusing to treat those whose advance directives indicated a preference for aggressive intervention. In 2020, for example, when many hospitals were inundated by COVID-19 patients, a number of states developed triage policies that allowed hospitals to ignore advance directives and, instead, base treatment decisions on the likelihood that patients would benefit.[72]

Why Do the Dead Need Rights?

Neither the dead nor, in many instances, the dying are aware of whatever rights they may have. The rights of the dead arise from the interests and concerns of the living. To begin with, the living fear death. Indeed, terror of death is a major driving force in human affairs.[73] In his epic verse *On the Nature of Things*, the great Roman epicurean philosopher Lucretius aptly observed that it was their fear of death that made human beings dependent upon religious and secular authorities and led them to accept superstitions and irrational beliefs that promised protection from death.[74]

In some measure, by granting rights to the dead, the living are addressing their own fear of the inevitable end of life. A regime of legislatively and judicially guaranteed posthumous rights functions as a legal "hereafter" in which property rights, privacy rights, and even reproductive rights continue to be protected. Perhaps this regime of posthumous rights might be seen as the contemporary equivalent of some ancient burial custom that allowed decedents to be buried with their possessions for possible use in the next world.[75] There was never a guarantee that entombed property would ever be useful to its deceased owners. But, as we have seen, posthumous property rights, moral rights, and so forth, effectively can be exercised from the grave—at least so long as the polity granting those rights continues to exist.

The rights of the dying are also important in this context. Sociologist Zygmunt Bauman observed that one strategy for confronting death, which he identifies as typical of the modern world, is to deconstruct it.[76] Death, in its totality, cannot be defeated, but particular aspects of death and dying can be addressed and death, thereby, rendered less terrifying. Consider the State of Maryland advance medical directive form (MOLST), which all state residents are encouraged to file. Individuals are asked whether and under what circumstances they wish to be resuscitated. They are given several options regarding artificial ventilation and artificially administered fluids and nutrition, as well as choices about a variety of other procedures. Bureaucratically, death is transformed from an unimaginable, horrifying totality into a lengthy and tedious checklist of options. Exercising their right to informed consent helps the living exorcize their terror of death.

Posthumous rights, moreover, allow living persons to know that they will be able to provide for people and things they care about after their own deaths. Decedents' wills are filled with provisions doling out money to children, institutions, and social causes. Wills and estates, as we saw above, frequently also include well-meaning, if sometimes misguided, efforts to ensure that beneficiaries will pay heed to their forbears' wisdom and guidance regarding such matters as marriage and charitable works.

Thus, the state allows the dead to exercise posthumous rights from a secular afterlife. This is one way in which Foucault's metaphysical border between life and death has been breached by governments and their laws. Another is the posthumous political power of the dead.

The Power of the Dead

According to the Hebrew Bible, the dead have neither an interest in nor power over the living. In *Kohelet* (Ecclesiastes) 9:5 and 9:6 the narrator, often identified as King Solomon, avers:

For the living know that they will die, but the dead know nothing, and they have no more reward, for their remembrance is forgotten. Also their love, as well as their hate, as well as their provocation has already been lost, and they have no more share forever in all that is done under the sun.[1]

A similar idea of posthumous indifference is advanced in Thornton Wilder's well-known play *Our Town*, where the Stage Manager declares:

You know as well as I do that the dead don't stay
interested in us living people for very long. Gradually, gradually,
   they

lose hold of the earth . . . and the ambitions they had . . . and the
    pleasures
they had . . . and the things they suffered . . . and the people
they loved.[2]

At the risk of simultaneously committing blasphemy and con-
tradicting the wise Mr. Wilder, I would suggest that the dead can
exercise quite a bit of influence over the world of the living. Perhaps
it is true that the dead lack sentience and "know nothing," but
premortem choices made by the dead certainly affect the world of the
living. As we saw in our discussion of testamentary rights, the living
possess antemortem interests in what will occur after their deaths and
may develop strategies to posthumously further their "ambitions"
and retain shares "in all that is done under the sun." Besides, even
among the living, do only the sentient exercise political influence? If
this was the case, electoral democracy could hardly function.[3] Indeed,
according to some accounts, posthumous voting remains common
in such jurisdictions as Cook County, Illinois, where the dead seem
to vote just like everyone else.[4]

The dead can exercise influence in several ways. First, they may
exercise considerable power through the act of dying itself. Second,
the dead can exercise influence simply by disappearing from the
world of the living. Third, the dead can exert posthumous influence
through social and political institutions they built while still living.
Finally, the dead can exercise power through monuments, paintings,
photos, films, written works, and videos they created or that were
created by others to memorialize them. Historian Pierre Nora called
memorial statuary *lieux de memoire* or places of memory. Through
statues, tombs, and other memorial sites, the dead can, indeed,
become so powerful that their living foes feel compelled to exorcize
their spirits and seek to permanently silence them. Let us consider,
in turn, each of these means through which the dead exercise power
among the living.

The Act of Dying

By dying, some individuals hope to have a posthumous effect on the world they are leaving. Some such persons are barely noticed and quickly forgotten, but others, like successful soldiers or the 9/11 suicide bombers, are able to exert considerable influence as they cross the border from this world to the next.

In his famous 1895 work *Suicide*, Emile Durkheim defined suicide as a death resulting from the act of the victim that he or she knows will produce this result. Durkheim distinguished between egoistic suicide and altruistic suicide, that is, suicide committed for personal reasons versus those committed to achieve some greater good.[5] Durkheim's definition was refined a bit by his one-time student and subsequent collaborator Maurice Halbwachs. Halbwachs thought that in discussing altruistic suicides Durkheim did not adequately distinguish between those who sought death and those willing to accept death if it became a necessary condition for the furtherance of some important posthumous goal. An example of the former might be the Buddhist ideal of deliberate self-sacrifice. The latter, according to Halbwachs, might be exemplified by "the soldier who reluctantly accepts death in order to take the enemy with him," or the ship's captain willing if necessary to go down with the sinking vessel in order to safeguard the lives of passengers and crew members.[6] In either case, though, the individuals in question view the loss of their own lives as necessary to bring about, or as justified by, some larger end whose achievement they themselves will not live to see. The goals for which individuals willingly sacrifice their lives vary. Some give their own lives to save strangers in what appear to be heroic and altruistic actions.[7] Others have been willing to sacrifice to promote secular ideologies like communism. The most common drivers of altruistic suicide, though, are religion and patriotism.

Religion

As to the first of these, religion is not organic; it is taught, but if internalized, religious belief can be a powerful force. Throughout recorded history individuals have willingly sacrificed their lives to contribute to the supereminence and propagation of their religious creeds. For some the goal may have been personal immortality. Durkheim would classify these as egoistical suicides. Others, however, seem to have been mainly concerned with the earthly glory of their religion and the honor accorded to their gods. Certainly every modern-day creed celebrates its martyrs—individuals who at the pain of death refused to betray their faith and died hoping that their actions would serve their gods and religious community.

Among Jews, martyrdom has generally been discouraged by religious authorities, though individuals willing to give their lives for the perpetuation of the faith are honored in Jewish prayer and ritual. The Maccabees are extolled as martyrs who refused to accept Greek rule and the Hellenic influences that challenged Hebrew culture and religious practices. For many Jews, Israelis in particular, an important expression of martyrdom in the defense of the Jewish faith is the speech that Jewish historian Flavius Josephus attributed to Eleazar Ben Yair, the leader of the Jewish Sicarii who continued to hold the fortress of Masada after the Romans defeated the Jewish army and destroyed Jerusalem in 70 AD. Eleazer explains to his troops that they must now die by their own hands to honor the glory of God.

> My loyal followers, long ago we resolved to serve neither the Romans nor any else but only God, who alone is the true and righteous Lord of men: now the time has come that bids us prove our determination by our deeds.[8]

Similarly, during the Crusades and later, during the Spanish Inquisition, when given the choice, some Jewish communities, albeit not all, chose death over conversion to Christianity. Death was to be preferred to the abandonment of the true faith.

Consider, too, the early history of Christianity. For more than three centuries, Christians in the Roman Empire were persecuted by imperial authorities for refusing to recognize the divinity of the emperor. Some Christians chose to die rather than renounce their faith, and some church leaders encouraged martyrdom. They believed that these deaths would serve the church's interests by demoralizing the civil authorities and impressing the populace with the Christians' fortitude and courage. Of course, some individuals renounced their faith to avoid torture and death, but many did not. As the number of martyrs grew, the commemoration of Christian martyrs became public events throughout the empire and presented a major challenge to Roman authorities.[9]

The second-century Christian writer Tertullian declared that martyrdom was essential to the growth of the Christian faith in Rome. "The oftener we are mown down by you," he wrote, "the more in number we grow; the blood of Christians is seed."[10] This idea was echoed centuries later by St. Thomas à Becket who was said to have declared to his murderers, "If all the swords in England were pointed against my head, your threats would not move me. I am ready to die for my Lord, that in my blood the Church may obtain liberty and peace."[11]

Even today, Evangelical missionaries willingly risk arrest, imprisonment, and murder by proselytizing in the Muslim world. In recent years, a number of U.S. Christian medical workers associated with Evangelical groups have been murdered while working in clinics in Afghanistan, Lebanon, and Yemen while simultaneously disseminating Christian beliefs among Muslim patients. Few Muslims have been converted by their efforts, but the Evangelical organizations that sponsor these medical missionaries are able to point to them as examples they hope will inspire the faithful.[12]

Though Islam nominally forbids suicide, it too boasts of individuals who have chosen death to protect and promote the faith. Support for the idea of self-sacrifice for the glory of God can be found in the Qur'an. "Whoever fights in the path of God, whether he be slain or victorious, We shall give him a vast reward" (4:74). In later literature, those who fight on behalf of Islam are called *shuhada' al-ma'raka* or battlefield martyrs, a form of death declared to be the noblest way to depart this life.[13] Radical Islamists point to these ideas to justify suicide bombings. Jihadists reject the term "suicide bombing" and insist that attacks carried out by individuals who use their own deaths to bring destruction to an enemy should be called, instead, "martyrdom operations."[14]

Religious beliefs, of course, play some role in the recruitment of the Muslim jihadi suicide bombers who have attacked U.S., Israeli, and other Western targets for the past two decades. As Robert Pape shows, however, suicide bombers are generally motivated more by secular than religious beliefs and goals. In an overwhelmingly Islamic society jihadists feel compelled to offer a religious justification for their actions even if religious fervor was not the underlying driving force. Pape asserts that suicide terrorists are mainly driven by nationalist goals, particularly a desire to drive foreign forces from their land. And, says Pape, suicide terrorism works.[15] Suicide bombers were able to attack Western targets that were not vulnerable to other weapons possessed by Islamic militants and, albeit to a limited degree, affected the behavior and policies of the target countries.

As to the suicide bombers themselves, Pape finds that they were, for the most part, ordinary individuals, neither sinister criminals nor religious fanatics. The bombers approached their tasks with a sense of mission, devoted months to study and planning, and viewed their assignments as soldierly duties. For example, Mohammed Atta, leader of the 9/11 hijackers, believed it was his duty to help end the West's humiliation of the Islamic world.[16] Atta, like most of the others, was willing to give his life for a better world and, in the act of dying, deliberately touched off a chain of events that had a lasting effect upon the world of the living. By dying, Atta posthumously furthered his earthly ambitions and beliefs.

Nationalism

The secular versus religious motivations of jihadists can be debated. A second group of individuals willing to give their lives to achieve some greater, albeit posthumous, good consists of those whose deaths are almost certainly inspired by nationalism or patriotism. As in the case of religion, throughout recorded history, some individuals—Japanese kamikaze pilots come immediately to mind—have been willing to sacrifice their own lives for the good or glory of their homeland. The Roman poet Horace wrote, "Dulce et decorum est pro patria mori" (How sweet and honorable it is to die for one's country).[17] In the United States, the same idea is captured by patriot Nathan Hale, who declared as he was about to be hanged by the British on September 22, 1776, "I only regret that I have but one life to lose for my country."[18]

This ideal if sacrificial patriotism is extolled in every nation's literature and films. In the United States, films have been made about the heroes of the Alamo who, at least according to legend, gave their lives in a hopeless battle against Mexican forces as well as Sergeant Alvin York who risked his life in a desperate fight against German forces.[19] In his Gettysburg Address, President Abraham Lincoln declared that the dead had given their nation the "last full measure of devotion." At the headquarters of the U.S. Central Intelligence Agency, a Memorial Wall in the lobby of the original headquarters building displays 133 stars, each one representing an employee who gave his or her life in the line of duty. The first CIA employee to be killed in the line of duty was Douglas Mackiernan who stayed behind to destroy cryptographic equipment when the U.S. consulate in Tihwa, China, was evacuated after the defeat of Chinese Nationalist forces. Mackiernan destroyed the sensitive equipment but was killed attempting to escape China.

Most Americans who gave their lives for their country were serving in the military or undertaking other dangerous missions. These individuals did not wish to die but accepted the risk of death as an aspect of their duty to the nation. If they died, the benefits of their actions would presumably be posthumous. The United States, like other nations, depends upon the willingness of its citizens to calculate that the nation is more important than their own lives and to endanger their lives in its defense. In the heat of battle, of course, soldiers are more likely to risk death for their comrades than for their nation, but it is a sense of duty to the nation that brings many, some with great enthusiasm, to the battlefield where their lives are placed in jeopardy.

Perhaps some citizens require no prompting to find the spark of patriotism, especially sacrificial patriotism, within themselves. But governments understand that heroic citizens are more likely to be made than born and turn to civic education and nationalistic propaganda to ignite the spark and fan the flames of patriotism, especially in wartime.

Teaching Citizens to Die for Their Country

The term "propaganda" simply refers to a campaign of information and ideas, whether true or false, designed to persuade some audience to support a particular cause or political leader. Similar information and idea campaigns used to promote products and services are usually called advertising. The word "propaganda" apparently derives from the Catholic Church's *Congregatio de propaganda fide* or Congregation for Propagating the Faith, established in 1622 to encourage the spread of Catholic teachings in non-Catholic realms.

The term "propaganda" has a negative connotation because of its association with Nazi Germany and Joseph Stalin's USSR. Accordingly, the U.S. government refers to its own propaganda efforts as "civic education" or "public information." In ancient times, long before the term was introduced, secular rulers made use of propaganda, mainly to bolster the morale of their own troops before battle and to attempt to unnerve the enemy forces facing them. Thus, for example, in the campaign against Athens during the fifth century BC, Spartan troops were told, "We must not then fall short of our fathers' standards, nor fail to live up to our own reputation. For, the whole of Hellas is eagerly watching this action of ours. . . . Think, too, of the glory, or, if events turn out differently, the shame which you will bring to your ancestors and to yourselves, and with all this in mind follow your leaders."[20]

In the seventeenth century, with the expanded use of printing presses and the development of copper plate that permitted posters to be quickly printed, propaganda could be aimed at a larger audience. This became evident during the Thirty Years War when the pen and the sword were said to have forged a "formidable alliance."[21] Much of the propaganda produced in the seventeenth and eighteenth centuries had an external rather than internal target. That is, government propaganda was aimed more at undermining the morale of the troops, supporters, and subjects of an opposing regime than rallying support among the government's own subjects.

In western Europe during the late eighteenth century, however, the advent of the citizen soldier led regimes to direct more of their propaganda efforts toward domestic than foreign audiences. This new direction in propaganda was first manifest in America, whose colonial governments relied exclusively on volunteer militia forces before, during, and after the Revolutionary War. Militiamen could not be compelled to fight and had to be persuaded. As a result, with the beginnings of the revolt against Britain colonial pamphleteers, newspaper editors, and others were long accustomed to the idea of appealing to public opinion to advance their cause.

Virtually every action of the royal government was presented in a negative light and its significance exaggerated by colonial publicists to inflame popular sentiment and bring recruits flocking to the revolutionary cause. Paul Revere's inflammatory cartoons of the "Boston Massacre," a minor event in which British troops fired on rioters, were circulated throughout the colonies to exemplify British brutality. Samuel Adams earned the title "master of the puppets" for his anti-British propaganda in the *Boston Gazette*. In the aftermath of the 1773 Boston Tea Party, Adams worked through the Boston Committee of Correspondence to flood the colonies with distorted news stories portraying the British as cruel occupiers of the helpless city of Boston. During the war itself, Tom Paine's propaganda treatises *Common Sense*, *American Crisis*, and *Rights of Man* were read by virtually every colonist. "These are the times that try men's souls," Paine wrote. "The summer soldier and the sunshine patriot will, in this crisis shrink from the service of his country. . . . Tyranny, like hell, is not easily conquered; yet we have this consolation with us, that the harder the conflict the more glorious the triumph."[22]

These American efforts prefigured the propaganda efforts of France's post-Revolutionary regimes. Besieged on all sides by the armies of the anti-French coalitions, and with the old royal army in disarray, the National Assembly called upon the French nation to come to the defense of the fatherland. The National Assembly created a Committee on Public Instruction, later replaced by the Committee on Public Safety, to rally the nation on behalf of the Revolution and the French nation. This committee issued posters and pamphlets and chose the iconic figure of "Marianne" as the symbol of French liberty, to be displayed on statues and posters throughout the nation. Propaganda agents were instructed to distribute patriotic pamphlets and journals, particularly the *Soiree de camp*, aimed at military units, and the *Bulletin*, an official government, mass-circulation daily newspaper, which was posted throughout the nation to present the regime's view of domestic and international events. The result of these efforts was a "nation in arms." As one observer put it, "A force appeared that beggared all imagination. Suddenly war again became the business of the people—a people of 30 millions, all of whom considered themselves to be citizens."[23] These French efforts became the models for state efforts to teach citizens the importance of being willing to die for their countries.

We might ask whether these efforts to persuade citizens to fight and, perhaps, die for their countries were successful. The answer is a resounding yes. During the First World War, the various combatants recruited some sixty million soldiers of whom fifteen million died in the service of their respective countries. In the Second World War, nearly three hundred million soldiers served and perhaps thirty million died. In the end, did the tens of millions who gave their lives matter? Did they exert power by dying? Collectively they did. The late historical sociologist Charles Tilly observed that today's states are the survivors of millennia of culling in which their weaker rivals were defeated or absorbed.[24] When Americans sacrificed in response to calls to "remember the Alamo," to avenge the "day of infamy" or the 9/11 terror attacks, as they died they collectively determined that their nation would not be among those culled.

The Departure of the Dead

A second way in which the dead exercise power is through the very fact of their passing from the world of the living. In a typical year, more than fifty million people die somewhere in the world, and each of these deaths is important to at least some among the living. Nearly all persons have some impact, be it large or small, positive or negative, upon their communities. The death of any individual almost certainly changes the lives of those left behind, albeit for better or worse. Perhaps, the impact may be felt primarily by close friends and family members. The death of a parent, for example, is likely to substantially reduce the life prospects and emotional well-being of their young children but possibly have only an ever-diminishing ripple effect beyond the immediate family circle.[25]

The death of an important public official or political leader, on the other hand, can have widespread and lasting consequences. Examples are numerous. The death of Richard III during the 1485 Battle of Bosworth Field prompted his Yorkist army to disintegrate and flee from a much smaller Tudor force, settling the question of who would rule England.[26] To take another example from English history, the beheading of Charles I in 1649 was an important step toward the establishment of British parliamentary democracy.[27] Or, to turn to Russian history, Vladimir Lenin's death in 1924 opened the way for Stalin's ruthless and murderous dictatorship, while Stalin's death in 1953 ended the ugliest chapter, at least to date, in modern Russian history. For better or worse, these deaths had powerful effects upon the world of the living. Indeed, one recent quantitative study indicates that between 1875 and 2004 the assassinations of some sixty national leaders had a significant effect upon the evolution of political institutions in the affected countries. One might only imagine how the history of the world would have changed if Adolph Hitler had not narrowly escaped assassination in 1939.[28]

The power of death is often amplified when many deaths co-occur. In human history, the largest numbers of deaths are associated with violence and disease, and in many instances such deaths have profoundly changed the course of human civilization. In the case of fatalities produced by war and violence, one hundred thousand deaths in the Revolutionary War made possible the creation of the United States of America. Perhaps five million deaths paved the way for the establishment of modern China. The collapse of Tsarist Russia and birth of the Soviet Union was midwifed by ten million deaths. The deaths of some six million Jews destroyed a one-thousand-year-old pillar of European civilization and brought about the creation of modern Israel.

As to disease, perhaps fifty million individuals, or 90 percent of the pre-Columbian indigenous population, died from diseases such as smallpox, measles, and plague brought to the New World by Europeans. These deaths opened the doors for the European conquest and settlement of the Americas.[29] In Europe, itself, more than one hundred million individuals died of plague between 1347 and 1351, reshaping western European economies and societies.[30] We do not yet know the full extent of the social, economic, and political consequences of the millions of deaths caused by COVID-19 in 2020 and 2021.

A Roman maxim held that the world is periodically purified and transformed by plague and war—*pestis et bellum*. Wielding these dread instruments, the Grim Reaper changes the world.

What the Dead Leave Behind

A third way that the dead exercise power in the world of the living is by leaving behind both material and nonmaterial works that will continue to affect the behavior, thought, and imaginations of the living. In most instances, perhaps, the ideas and attainments of the departed are soon forgotten. In other cases, though, a decedent's influence can persist for generations and even increase with the passage of time. As we saw above, several of America's founders saw in the writings of Francis Bacon a guide to immortality through the construction of political institutions through which their ideas might continue to govern the nation even as their bodies turned to dust.

Were the framers incorrect? Once brought into being, laws, constitutions, and government agencies can remain in existence for decades, even centuries, furthering the ideas and goals of individuals long dead. Whenever a court declares an act of some current Congress "unconstitutional," the long-dead hands of James Madison and the other framers of the U.S. Constitution are reaching from their graves to influence the lives of living Americans. Madison, indeed, strongly believed that the living should pay heed to the views of the dead. In a letter to Thomas Jefferson, Madison averred, "The improvements made by the dead form a debt against the living, who take the benefit of them. This debt cannot be otherwise discharged than by a proportionate obedience to the will of the Authors of the improvements."[31]

Like the Constitution, government bureaucracies can be seen as incarnations of the dead. Once established, bureaucracies tend to embody the ideas and goals of their creators as codified in their organic statutes and in the ideals and perspectives of the early leaders who established the agencies' operating cultures. Political scientist James Q. Wilson observed, "Every organization has a culture . . . a persistent, patterned way of thinking about the central tasks of and human relationships within an organization. Culture is to an organization what personality is to an individual . . . it is passed from one generation to the next. It changes slowly, if at all."[32] Agency cultures are typically born with agencies' original missions, the personalities of their early leaders, and the character of their earliest supporters. Once established, agency cultures can be remarkably resistant to change as agencies recruit employees and executives thought to be sympathetic to the agency's values and, for good measure, subject them to a lengthy process of training and indoctrination.

Many agencies seem incredibly dedicated to missions defined long ago. The U.S. Fish and Wildlife Service (USFWS), for example, was created in the nineteenth century to protect and conserve the nation's animal species and does so today, generally disregarding other economic and social interests. In recent years the USFWS has worked to return wolves and grizzly bears to the Northwest, even though these animals represent an economic and even physical threat to individuals engaged in ranching and recreational pursuits in the region.[33] Often, a cataclysmic event is required to alter an agency's long-established culture or sense of mission. For example, during the early 1980s the U.S. Coast Guard, which viewed itself as a quasi-military force, finally accepted the idea that boating safety and environmental protection were within the scope of its mission, but only after the agency was moved from the Treasury Department to the Department of Transportation, and then to the Department of Homeland Security, provided with new leadership, given a new statutory base, and subjected to several presidential orders.[34]

All agencies, civilian as well as military, are almost certain to resist efforts to compel them to undertake activities that are foreign to their institutional cultures and, thus, seem to pose a threat to their institutional autonomy or internal balance of power. Organizational theorist Harold Seidman wrote that attempts to compel agencies to engage in such activities are usually futile. "Alien transplants," he avers, "seldom take root" and are continually "threatened with rejection."[35] For example, numerous congressional efforts to compel the Federal National Mortgage Association (Fannie Mae), a quasi-public government-sponsored enterprise, to provide loans to low-income families have failed to affect the agency's behavior. Despite its public charter, Fannie Mae conceives itself to be a commercial enterprise with a duty to operate in as profitable a manner as possible. Loans to poor borrowers who lack credit worthiness do not comport with this sense of mission and are constantly—and successfully—resisted by the agency in spite of congressional pressure.[36]

James Madison, quoted above, thought this form of governance by the dead was appropriate. We might, however, pay heed to Friedrich Nietzsche, who warned that the agencies of the state were the "coldest of cold monsters."[37] Incarnations of the dead, such agencies lack the moral sensibilities of living humans. They are, in effect, without souls and for reasons of their own—"reasons of state"—will not hesitate to undertake oppressive, cruel, or violent actions, feeling no more concern than would any other soulless machine.

Take the matter of violence. At first blush, it may seem odd to link violence and bureaucracy. After all, the literal meaning of bureaucracy is a government of desks, and these desks are often occupied by the blandest and most mild-mannered functionaries. More than any other form of social organization, however, bureaucracy makes large-scale and long-term violence possible. Echoing Jean-Jacques Rousseau, Hannah Arendt once said that all humans had a feeling of animal pity for the suffering of others.[38] Perhaps Arendt was too optimistic and overlooked the fact that some individuals seem to have no moral compass. But many do, and indeed, in the famous experiments by Stanley Milgram, reported in his book *Obedience to Authority*, a number of subjects found the instructions they were given, which gave them the (false) impression that they were inflicting pain upon a volunteer, morally objectionable and refused to carry them out on those grounds. One subject, declining to continue, said, "Surely you've considered the ethics of this thing."[39]

Bureaucracy, however, undermines the moral limit of violence in at least three important ways. First, violence undertaken by bureaucratic organizations separates many of the actors from the ultimate act. Contractors and employees who labor in the weapons factories or offices of an army's extended tail, for example, do not directly confront whatever moral choices must be made by those in the front lines. As Zygmunt Bauman observes, such individuals seldom "face the moment of choice and face the consequences of their deeds."[40] Even if shown such consequences they can declare them to be unanticipated and unintended by them. Second, through the division of labor, bureaucratic organization breaks violent processes into small parts with each perpetrator undertaking only a fragment of the whole. The bureaucracy as a whole may be engaged in murder, but each individual, particularly those at a distance from the ultimate act, is responsible for only a portion of the task. One collects data, one works at a lathe, one repairs a generator. Taken by itself, each task is morally neutral. Finally, bureaucratic organization transfers moral responsibility from the actor to some abstract authority, which absolves the actor of blameworthiness. A number of Nazi officials accused of war crimes famously declared that they were "just carrying out orders" (*Befehl ist Befehl*) and bore no personal moral responsibility for the actions mandated by those orders. For these several reasons, we can agree with Bauman that bureaucracies adiaphorize social action, seeming to make it neither good nor bad—thus effectively eliminating the moral limits of violence.[41]

Since the publication of Arendt's account of the trial of Adolph Eichmann, the issue of bureaucracy and morality has been much discussed. This discussion, however, is often freighted by the enormity of the Holocaust, which tends to become not only an example, but *the* example of the ways in which bureaucracies marginalize moral concerns and render them irrelevant to the operations of the organization. The danger of this focus on one powerful example is that the adiaphoric impact of bureaucracy on social action becomes conflated with Nazism and accordingly viewed as an aberration rather than understood as a characteristic of all bureaucracies. Consider an American bureaucracy that today employs more than five hundred thousand Americans, not German Nazis. This bureaucracy, or complex of bureaucracies, is the U.S. penal system, a set of institutions that typically houses more than two million individuals, mainly men, who have been sentenced for various crimes or are in jail awaiting a formal disposition of their cases. While in the custody of America's prison bureaucracies many tens of thousands of the male inmates and a smaller number of women are subjected to violent, appalling, and disgusting treatment. In particular, many tens of thousands are sexually assaulted while incarcerated, usually by other inmates. Among the men, some are assaulted repeatedly, badly injured, and infected with the HIV virus—often a death sentence.

Of course, unlike the various German institutions dedicated to bringing about the Final Solution, U.S. carceral bureaucracies are not formally assigned to the task of promoting the rape of inmates. Indeed, neither the judges who sentence individuals to prison nor the guards and wardens who supervise them are usually the actual perpetrators of sexual assaults. Perhaps we should not consider them as blameworthy as the violent inmates who actually commit the bulk of the rapes. But if a man thoughtlessly and repeatedly pushes helpless individuals into cages containing savage beasts and carelessly locks the door and looks away, who is responsible for the result—the ravenous beasts or the indifferent man?

The law enforcement officials, judges, and jailers who control U.S. prisons usually commit no acts of violence themselves but do tolerate and seem indifferent to tens of thousands of cruel and violent acts committed in their institutions on a daily basis. Their indifference, moreover, exemplifies the three ways in which bureaucracy undermines the moral limits of violence. First, within the bureaucratic structure of the prison regime the various carceral officials are separated from the ultimate acts of violence their conduct promotes and can declare those acts to have been unanticipated and unintended by them. Second, the bureaucratic structure of the prison divides violent processes into small parts—the sentence, the transport, the cell assignment, the daily schedule, and so forth—each of which seems morally neutral. Finally, prison officials have no difficulty transferring moral responsibility for their actions elsewhere: lawmakers who enact sentencing laws and set prison funding levels, regulatory agencies that govern prison procedures, even the general public some of whose members clamor for harsh sentences and respond favorably to late-night television comedians who joke about prison rape.[42]

If confronted in court with allegations that their conduct tolerated and permitted violent rape, prison officials customarily rely upon all three of these bureaucratic responses. And, to confirm the adiaphoric character of bureaucracy, U.S. courts generally accept their reasoning. The legal standard applied by the courts in cases of prison rape is known as "deliberate indifference." According to this standard, prison officials have liability for a rape committed in their institutions only if they knew that particular rape was likely to take place and, nevertheless, decided not to take action. Officials easily prevail in almost all cases by arguing that the particular rape in question was unanticipated, that each of their actions, viewed individually, was perfectly appropriate, and that they adhered fully to all prison rules and regulations. *Herr Oberst* Eichmann could not have presented a better statement of bureaucratic inculpability.

Thus, in these ways, Nietzsche was correct and Madison wrong. The bureaucracies of the state, incarnations of the dead, are indeed the coldest of cold monsters.

Memorials

A fourth way in which the dead exercise power is through icons, visual images, literary works, and other memorials. A statue of a famous but now deceased person is not primarily a work of art. It is, rather, an attempt to express in the present the values and ideals associated with that individual, and to recommend these as having continuing validity despite the death of the person so memorialized. Many U.S. statues memorialize the nation's heroes and leaders. In the case of the larger memorials—the Washington Monument, Lincoln Memorial, and so forth—tour guides and pamphlets are available to explain the significance of the person and the importance of his or her words, deeds, and ideas. School groups study the monuments and learn from them. Through such memorials, the dead continue to exert influence.

The fact that the dead can exert influence through memorials explains the battle over statues that broke out in the United States during the past several years. The chief focus of this battle was the seven hundred or so monuments to heroes of the Confederacy scattered throughout the United States. Most of these statues were built during the late nineteenth and early twentieth centuries—the majority around 1900—with the purpose of presenting Southern secession, the Confederacy, and even slavery as just and heroic.

Similarly, pre–World War II academic history and school texts, dominated by the so-called Dunning school, emphasized the unreadiness or incapacity of newly freed Blacks to exercise political rights, excoriated Northern Radical Republicans for imposing "Negro rule" upon the prostrate South, and applauded the efforts of white

Southerners to reclaim their rightful political supremacy in the region.[43] Generations of students learned a historical narrative that gave legitimacy to the South's apartheid system and to policies of racial discrimination in such realms as housing and employment in the North. The statues honoring the heroes of the Confederacy gave material expression to these ideas, indeed, carved them in granite or cast them in bronze.

During the past several years, of course, the Black Lives Matter movement and other groups have demanded the destruction of the Confederate statues, asserting that they represent racist ideas that have no place in contemporary America. After a battle over statues in Virginia, former Virginia governor Terry McAuliffe declared that the Confederate monuments should be torn down because they celebrated "insidious policies" and helped to keep racism alive in present-day institutions and attitudes. Former president Donald Trump, for his part, averred that those attempting to remove the monuments were seeking to rewrite history in order to remove all traces of ideas with which they disagreed and, in so doing, hoped to change contemporary political culture. In essence, Trump and McAuliffe agreed on the power of the statues, but Trump thought their message was an important one while McAuliffe believed that the statues and the ideas they represented should be eradicated.

Of course, the dead do not always need imposing granite or marble statues to speak. Think of the power exerted by the grainy cell phone image of George Floyd as he died at the hands of a police officer. Yet there is something especially powerful about a statue. When the dead live in granite or bronze their power is amplified, their voices heard through the centuries before inevitably being stilled.

The Enduring Power of the Dead

The idea of posthumous influence may, at first blush, appear peculiar. Yet, as they die, through the institutions they have built and though memorials the dead do exert posthumous influence over the living. And sometimes the dead are very powerful. Consider the example of the sacred mummies of the Inca empire. After destroying the military power of the Aztec and Inca empires, Spanish conquistadors made a determined effort to suppress the religious institutions and beliefs that played central roles in the lives of their new subjects. The elimination of indigenous religious practices and the forcible conversion of native populations to Roman Catholicism was viewed by the Spaniards as an important step in the pacification of their new possessions. By destroying the natives' holy places and religious symbols and replacing them with their own churches, priests, and icons, the Spaniards sought to affirm the moral superiority of European civilization as well as to deprive their new subjects of a potential rallying point for continued resistance.

In the case of the Incas, resistance continued for many years after Francisco Pizarro hanged the Inca emperor Atahualpa and attempted to install a puppet regime through which the Spaniards hoped to govern the empire. As an important element of their resistance to Spanish rule, members of the Inca nobility or *panaqa* endeavored to protect their empire's most important religious symbols, particularly including the mummified remains of former emperors, widely venerated as sacred objects who, in imperial times, posthumously owned land and slaves and were brought to attend important meetings and functions. Members of the *panaqa* endured death by torture at the hands of the Spaniards to prevent these sacred mummies from falling into Spanish hands.[44] The Spaniards, for their part, viewed the mummies as a severe threat to their own power and hunted for them for nearly three decades before finding and destroying the last of them. In essence, the dead were so powerful that they had to be killed again.

CHAPTER 5

Oblivion

For the favored dead, the state offers a secular afterlife from which decedents exercise posthumous rights and influence in the world of the living. Some of the favored dead are accorded honors long after their demise—funeral ceremonies and splendid monuments.

Not all the dead, however, are seen as virtuous or worthy of regard. These disfavored dead include paupers, the inmates of prisons and psychiatric hospitals, and the enemy dead. The disfavored dead of an earlier era—sinners and heretics—were barred from the churchyard and from heaven. Today's disfavored dead are interred without ceremony in unmarked graves.

Decedents who are especially reviled may be unceremoniously consigned to oblivion. For example, the body of terrorist Osama Bin Laden, mastermind of the 9/11 terror attacks, was thrown into the sea from the deck of a U.S. warship for fear that a marked grave would become a shrine for his followers. In an even more extreme

case, a state may endeavor to erase all genetic trace of those they kill,
The Nazis, for example, were not content to consign the bodies and
cremains of Jews to unmarked mass graves. The entire Jewish race
was to be sent to oblivion.

William Shakespeare saw a certain democracy in death. Rich
and poor, king and beggar, all became food for the worms. "Not
where he eats, but where he is eaten," says Hamlet to Claudius. "A
certain convocation of politic worms are e'en at him. Your worm is
your only emperor for diet: we fat all creatures else to fat us, and we
fat ourselves for maggots: your fat king and your lean beggar is but
variable service—two dishes, but to one table: that's the end" (*Hamlet*,
act 4, scene 3).

Shakespeare notwithstanding, the contemporary treatment of the
dead seems to recapitulate the social and political stratifications of
life rather than to reflect any democratic tendencies. To begin with,
not all deaths are viewed as equally significant. When a prominent
individual dies, the event receives a good deal of attention from the
media. Lengthy, sometimes prewritten obituaries are published in
leading newspapers; television commentators discuss the significance
of the death; and other persons of importance offer reflections on the
decedent's life. Events to commemorate the individual's passing and
an elaborate funeral may be held. Friends and relatives will deliver
eulogies celebrating the life and work of the decedent. Some of these
eulogies become famous in their own right. One example is Ted
Kennedy's eulogy for his murdered brother, Robert. Paraphrasing
George Bernard Shaw, Kennedy said,

> My brother need not be idealized, or enlarged in death beyond what
> he was in life; to be remembered simply as a good and decent man,
> who saw wrong and tried to right it, saw suffering and tried to heal
> it, saw war and tried to stop it. Those of us who loved him and who
> take him to his rest today, pray that what he was to us and what he
> wished for others will some day come to pass for all the world. As he
> said many times, in many parts of this nation, to those he touched
> and who sought to touch him: Some men see things as they are and
> say why; I dream things that never were and say why not.[1]

Following journalistic custom, obituaries and eulogies are seldom critical of prominent decedents. The rule is to speak no ill of the dead. Thus, for example, when Britain's Prince Philip died in 2021, newspaper accounts focused on his dedication to public service and ignored Philip's occasionally racist comments.[2] Obituaries of Richard Nixon mentioned the misdeeds that forced the former president to resign but gave more emphasis to his accomplishments, especially in the realm of foreign policy. Obituaries and other memorial commemorations help to extend the life of the decedent and symbolically forestall death.[3]

The death of an average, middle-class American is usually noted by a brief newspaper obituary, which provides a sketch of the person's life and lists the decedent's grieving family members. If the death is considered newsworthy, an obituary is written by a newspaper staffer. If not, the obituary is usually written by a funeral director and paid for by the family. Newspapers are happy to publish lengthy paid obituaries since they charge by the column inch.[4] In death, as in life, the rich often receive more attention than their actual deeds might seem to merit. Decedents who were poor or had no families to mourn their passing usually must make their way to the grave without mention in any newspaper or other publication. Those who were anonymous in life remain so in death.

Places of burial generally seem to reflect the social structures of the world of the living.[5] In most nations, heroic figures are interred in special places reserved for the most meritorious dead. These include America's Arlington National Cemetery, China's Babaoshan Revolutionary Cemetery, and Russia's Kremlin Wall Necropolis. Of course, great national heroes like George Washington, Mao Zedong, and Vladimir Lenin have their own burial places where their remains rest in splendid repose where they can receive the homage of grateful citizens. These individuals have achieved the immortality granted by fame.

A step below the burial sites of the nation's great figures, wealthy individuals might occupy places in family crypts or mausoleums or, if they prefer cremation, in elaborate above-ground columbaria. These are the thanatotic equivalents of the large homes in which members of this stratum spent their lives—and suggest a reluctance to mingle with the hoi polloi even in death. Some older urban cemeteries contain a jumble of crypts and mausoleums while newer, more capacious cemeteries on the outskirts of urban areas provide room for a better spacing of these often imposing monuments. These mausoleums, like the tombs of the great, bespeak influence. And it is not hard to imagine that their occupants might wield power after death. Most, indeed, continue to influence the world of the living through testamentary trusts.

In the United States, still a further step down in the funerary class structure is the commonplace lawn cemetery that houses the remains of most middle- and working-class Americans. Like everything in middle America, lawn cemeteries vary in cost and, accordingly, in levels of upkeep and quality of funerary amenities. Thus, the dead rest in neighborhoods similar to the ones in which they lived. And just as some members of the nobility once considered it inappropriate to demand burial inside the church, some wealthy Americans consider elaborate funerals and large mausoleums gauche and prefer simple headstones, albeit made of the finest materials.[6]

In these cemeteries, decedents are typically buried in neat rows marked by small headstones or horizontal plaques on which their names and some pertinent facts such as dates of birth and death are engraved. The headstones may be concrete, marble, or granite and perhaps decorated with brass filigree. Lawn cemeteries are generally designed to facilitate visitation. Guests can obtain cemetery maps at the gatehouse to help them find their way to the appropriate grave. Wide pathways allow friends and relatives to drive and park close to the grave site. On a warm Sunday afternoon, groups of visitors might walk about, mingling with the dead and communing with their late loved ones. Visitors often bring flowers and exchange recollections of the deceased, while some speak to the dead as though their words might be heard in the next world. Other visitors seek inspiration from their memories of the departed. Such cemeteries seem to allow the dead to linger on for a time in the ersatz afterlife from which the favored dead continue to be a presence in the world of the living.

Despite the growing popularity of cremation, most cremains are buried in a cemetery or columbarium rather than scattered.

The Potter's Field

Alas, not all the departed are treated with such respect and dignity. The disposition of unclaimed and unidentified bodies is a growing problem in the United States. Each year, some one hundred thousand bodies are unclaimed, and of these, roughly 15 percent are unidentified. These numbers have been growing because of deaths associated with America's opioid and covid-19 epidemics.[7]

According to a recent study, the unclaimed dead consist largely of individuals from the margins of U.S. society, often sick, poor, and isolated. Most lived alone in rented residences or hotel rooms. Some had been dead for weeks before their decomposing bodies were discovered because neighbors or passersby complained of an offensive odor. Many had histories of drug or alcohol abuse.[8] With the recent rise in homelessness, the unclaimed or unidentified dead are often likely to be found in homeless encampments or lying in the street. Or take the recent case of the Sangamon County, California, homeless man found crushed to death when the contents of the dumpster in which he had been sleeping were deposited into a garbage truck and compacted.[9] Even when they can be identified, the unclaimed often have no next of kin who can be found. And, perhaps more often, those relatives who can be traced are unable or unwilling to take responsibility for the remains. Funerals, which can cost several thousand dollars, are too expensive for some to afford, and in many cases, such issues as drug abuse and mental illness had left the unclaimed individuals estranged from their families long before their deaths. One Maricopa County, Arizona, official said, "We've had some people say, 'I'm glad they're dead. . . . I hope they burn in Hell.'"[10]

Some U.S. cities make use of taxpayer-funded cemeteries where unclaimed or unidentified individuals are buried. Such cemeteries are sometimes known as "potter's fields." The term is derived from the New Testament account of the burial ground of *Akeldama*, used for the interment of strangers and indigents. The land had previously served as a source of the high quality red clay employed by local potters for the production of ceramics. According to the Gospel of Matthew, the priests of Jerusalem purchased the burial ground with the thirty pieces of silver that had been paid to Judas for betraying Jesus.

America's largest and best-known potter's field is Hart Island, New York, a mile-long strip of land in Long Island Sound, accessible only by boat. Since the 1860s, Hart Island has served as New York City's main public cemetery. The first persons buried on Hart Island were several hundred captured Confederate soldiers from a group of several thousand in a military prison on the island. The soldiers succumbed to chronic diarrhea and pneumonia, results of the harsh living conditions to which they were subjected. Soon, these first to be interred were joined by new corpses from the city's busy morgue.[11]

Today, roughly 1,500 persons are buried on the island each year. This number may increase in times when diseases such as AIDS or COVID-19 produce higher mortality rates in the city, especially among the indigent for whom Hart Island is a final resting place. Those buried on the island generally include quite a number of children, infants, and stillborn babies, along with more than a few amputated limbs and dismembered body parts sometimes found in the city. The island is currently said to be the burial site for nearly one million persons, though the precise number is not known since a fire in 1977 destroyed nearly a century of records.

The dead of Hart Island are interred without a ceremony and placed in pine coffins that are lowered into trenches in groups of 150. Each group consists of two rows, each three coffins deep. Babies are also interred in trenches but in groups of 100, consisting of twenty rows, each five coffins deep. Each of these trenches is marked by a concrete pillar that identifies it as a burial place but does not name any of the persons it holds. Over the decades, the trenches have been excavated every twenty-five to forty years to make room for new generations of occupants when the remains of the current group have had an opportunity to fully decompose.[12]

At least in recent years, each coffin has been numbered and a corresponding record made of the decedent's approximate age, ethnicity, gender, and the place where the body was found. The person's name is recorded if known. These records are kept by the New York prison system. The most recent burial records include DNA, fingerprints, and photographs kept by the Office of the Chief Medical Examiner. Body parts are not recorded and are simply buried in boxes labeled "limbs." Using the official records, relatives are able to identify a handful of bodies each year. Some of these are disinterred and sent elsewhere for burial. The occasional individual wishing to visit a relative's grave will find it difficult to reach Hart Island. There is no general public access to the island, and visits must be scheduled in advance for a specific two-hour time slot. Plans announced in 2021 call for better access to the island, but no time frame has been developed.[13] Thus far, the dead of Hart Island have not been deemed worthy of visitors.

On Hart Island, the dead receive a burial and an identification number in an official database. But even this perfunctory treatment is not accorded to most of the nation's unclaimed dead. With the exception of veterans, whose burials are handled by the Department of Veterans' Affairs, the United States has no national system for dealing with the bodies of the dead. State laws and local practices vary enormously.

The laws of some states allow unclaimed bodies to be sent to medical schools for physician training and dissection. Until recent years, some hospitals engaged in an illicit trade in cadavers. Unclaimed bodies were sold by unscrupulous hospital morgue attendants and cemetery officials to medical schools for research and study before they could even reach the local potter's field for burial. For example, in 1887, the city of Omaha, Nebraska, purchased a plot of land for the interment of paupers, deceased prisoners, and unidentified decedents. Over the next decades, undertakers charged with transporting and burying corpses at this potter's field occasionally made some extra cash by selling the bodies to medical students. In some cases, the undertakers would reportedly make a show of burying the bodies in shallow graves during the day and then fill in the holes after the medical students removed the corpses after dark.[14] To end this abuse, most states enacted Anatomy Acts setting legal frameworks for medical school use of unclaimed cadavers. Accordingly, today in some cities and counties unclaimed bodies can be lawfully sent to medical schools by the local coroner or medical examiner. However, other states, including New York, prohibit the practice. Many schools, moreover, will not accept unclaimed cadavers for fear of subsequent complaints from relatives who had been unaware of the dispositions of their family member's remains.

Most localities do not allocate funds for actual funerals for unclaimed bodies and have developed inexpensive procedures for dealing with them. In Los Angeles County, for example, unclaimed bodies are cremated, and the cremains stored in the coroner's office for three years. At the end of this period, the cremains are buried in trenches in groups of one thousand with a single marker indicating the group's year of death. The county sponsors an annual interfaith ceremony for its unclaimed decedents. In Detroit, the county medical examiner's office stores unclaimed bodies in a refrigerated semitrailer in its parking lot, periodically contracting with a funeral director to dispose of the bodies. These are unceremoniously buried in mass graves. Cemetery workers have generally "dug up a trench and lined up the body bags." In North Carolina, unclaimed bodies are cremated and the ashes scattered at sea. In Jacksonville, Florida, unclaimed bodies are cremated and the ashes scattered over a common grave. Dallas, Texas, considered liquefying remains through a process called alkaline hydrolysis that reduces a corpse to a brownish liquid. Though the process is said to be environmentally friendly, some Dallas City Council members expressed revulsion at the idea.[15]

The District of Columbia's medical examiner holds bodies for thirty days. If they are unclaimed, the bodies are turned over to a private funeral home that has a contract with the city to cremate the corpses and bury the cremains in marked graves less than fifty miles outside the city. In actuality, most cremains are buried in two vaults in an unmarked location in a Baltimore cemetery. Those buried before 2013 were sent to a historically Black cemetery in Arlington, Virginia, where they were also deposited in an unmarked buried vault. The cremains are contained in small boxes within the vault. The boxes bear only paper name tags, and after a few years in the damp soil, no specific set of cremated remains is identifiable.[16] Neither cemetery is mentioned on the district's website, so a relative might have difficulty determining in what cemetery a family member was buried, much less the particular grave. The suburban lawn cemeteries of the middle classes are places of remembrance. The unclaimed bodies of the poor, on the other hand, are sent to burial places where they can more quickly be forgotten.

Psychiatric Facilities

Another group of unclaimed decedents are the dead of U.S. psychiatric hospitals. These individuals were not simply forgotten but were often deliberately put out of mind. Until recent years, individuals committed to psychiatric facilities typically lived out their lives in the hospitals, fading gradually from the society of the living. In some respects, they died long before they were buried.

In the nineteenth and early twentieth centuries, those adjudged to be mentally ill often were involuntarily committed, often at the behest of family members, to public psychiatric hospitals. More than 250 of these institutions were built in the United States.[17] Those committed included children who had been deemed incorrigible or were simply unruly and women who persistently disobeyed their husbands. Over the decades, several million persons lived in these usually crowded state institutions where they might perform menial tasks and, in some cases, be subjected to questionable treatments such as shock therapy, prefrontal lobotomies, and branding with hot irons, ostensibly to bring patients to their senses. Most of these psychiatric hospitals are closed today, but as recently as the 1950s, more than half a million Americans were confined to state mental institutions.[18]

During their lengthy stays, many inmates of psychiatric hospitals received no visitors. Some inmates had no families, and those who did were often abandoned by families that wanted to escape the

stigma of a relative with mental illness. The hospitals themselves
discouraged visitors and saw inmates' attachments to the outside
world as a threat to the total control they sought to exercise over
inmates' lives.[19]

The isolation of the inmates that began with their commitment
continued after death. Each of America's psychiatric hospitals
included a cemetery where deceased inmates could be buried in
unmarked graves. In 2013, for example, thousands of unidentifiable
bodies were found beneath the grounds of what had been the
Mississippi State Insane Asylum that closed in 1935 after housing
the state's mentally ill for eight decades. The hospital's death rate
was high, and decedents had been unceremoniously buried in
unmarked graves.[20] In a similar vein, several thousand unidentified
graves were found on the grounds of the now-shuttered Austin State
Farm School Colony in Texas. Opened in 1933 and noted for its use
of shock therapy and lobotomies, for more than a century Austin
State served as a facility for mentally disabled boys. The graveyard
of the Central Islip Psychiatric Center in New York State includes
the graves of a number of Holocaust survivors. These nameless
decedents often had been assigned two numbers—one tattooed on
their forearms by the Nazis and another on their headstones by the
psychiatric hospital.[21] Nearly two thousand graves with crumbling
numbered headstones remain on the campus of the defunct Athens
Lunatic Asylum in Ohio.[22] At the Athens asylum, as at the others,
if marked at all, graves were numbered rather than named to spare
families the shame of association with a mentally ill member. Thus,
even more than the poor, those deemed to be insane were separated
from society in death as they had been in life.

Of course, the United States is not the only nation whose psychiatric hospitals have consigned their dead to limbo. The psychiatric
institutions overseen by French local governments usually included
their own "cemeteries of the lunatics," which collectively hold thousands of unmarked, often unrecorded, grave sites. Often bodies
were buried two or three to a coffin. The psychiatric asylums were
considered to be places of exclusion, and their graveyards are now
called "cemeteries of the forgotten."[23]

Also left to decompose in unmarked graves are the bodies of thousands of children around the world who lived in inhumane conditions in orphanages or in such institutions as Canada's Indian boarding schools. At the latter, the institutional goal was to separate children from their families and root out all traces of their own culture. Sometimes cultural genocide led to brutality and even murder when children proved resistant. The bodies were buried without markers and sometimes in mass graves.[24] Here, too, the conditions of death echoed the conditions of life.

Recently, the U.S. Department of the Interior admitted that perhaps tens of thousands of Native American, Native Alaskan, and Native Hawaiian children died while in the custody of federal Indian boarding schools between 1819 and 1969. These schools were intended to assimilate the children and erase their native roots. The graves of the decedents are unmarked and forgotten.[25]

Death in Prison

Another institution that often boasts its own burial ground is the prison. For the dead of U.S. prisons, a lonely burial is just one more condition of punishment and, as in the case of the psychiatric inmates, the culmination of years or even decades of incarceration during which they gradually fade from the memories of the living. Death is a gradual process rather than an abrupt ending.

Many state prison systems include a cemetery, and the federal Bureau of Prisons maintains a cemetery at the Fort Leavenworth, Kansas, federal prison. According to the federal government's Bureau of Justice Statistics, between 2001 and 2019 about sixty-five thousand inmates died in the nation's state prisons.[26] During the same period, another seven thousand died in federal custody and perhaps as many as eighteen thousand more in local jails. Of the state prisoners, nearly 90 percent died of heart disease, cancer, liver disease, and AIDS-related conditions. In 2020, covid-19 became a significant cause of death in prisons and jails. Homicide and suicide rates among state prisoners were twice those in the general population.

Though the precise numbers are difficult to determine, the bodies of many thousands of deceased prison inmates are buried in such places as Alabama's Limestone Correctional Facility cemetery, Florida's Union Correctional Facility cemetery, and Texas's Captain Joe Byrd Cemetery in Huntsville, which serves the state's Huntsville Prison. Families generally have the right to claim the bodies of inmates who die in custody, but this right is seldom exercised. Long-serving inmates have generally lost touch with family members; inmate families are often too poor to attend, much less pay for, a funeral; and, in some cases, family members are themselves incarcerated at the time of the inmate's death. Thus, when Earnest Arrington Hubbard died of kidney disease in 2003 while serving a life sentence at St. Clair Correctional Facility in Alabama, his son, Earnest Akeem was unable to take possession of his father's remains. Akeem was at the time himself incarcerated on a fraud conviction at the Federal Correctional Institution in Talladega, Alabama. "When I called, they said they took him to a grave at Limestone [Prison cemetery]. If nobody come get you, if you ain't got no money and don't nobody care, they throw you up there," Akeem said.[27]

Throughout the prison system, graveyards are filled with often unidentified, forgotten individuals who are interred after brief burials conducted by fellow inmates. At Arkansas's infamous Cummins Prison Farm, the unidentified bodies of as many as two thousand individuals were once found in unmarked graves. The men appeared to have died violently, whether at the hands of prison authorities or fellow inmates could not be ascertained.[28] At Texas's largest prison cemetery, for more than a century, no records were kept of the names of decedents. Men entered the prison and never returned.[29] In Florida's prison cemetery—which itself has no name—deceased inmates have been buried since the nineteenth century. In recent years, the leading cause of death has been AIDS, often acquired as a result of prison rape, a widespread problem in U.S. correctional institutions. For many decades, graves were marked by license tags, produced by a prison license plate factory, noting only the decedent's prison inmate number and date of death. Today's license tags also indicate the individual's name. "We used to have just a number on the marker," said prison chaplain Eldon Cornett. "When I came here in the 1970s, several of us thought it was not really a good idea to send a man off to eternity with just a number. So we've been trying to rectify that."[30] Beneath the upscale Houston, Texas, suburb of Sugar Land is a forgotten burial yard containing the unmarked graves of an undetermined number of African American convict laborers who, in the nineteenth century, worked in the sugar plantations that subsequently gave the city its name. Convicts labored under brutal conditions. Those who died were thrown into quickly dug unmarked graves.[31]

Life and death are sometimes viewed as binary possibilities: an individual is either alive or dead. Yet intermediate stages do exist. Some prison inmates begin to die long before they are given a quick burial and an unmarked grave. In some parts of the world, prisoners are routinely beaten, tortured, starved, and otherwise abused by their jailers. Such unfortunates are not quite dead, but neither are they alive. They briefly exist in an intermediate state of suspended animation separate from the living and waiting to join the dead. Mbembe aptly calls this intermediate state the death world.[32]

In the German concentration camps of the mid-twentieth century, individuals living in this near-death state were known as *Muselmanner*. These were inmates who had been brutalized to the point of death and had given in to a form of torpor and apathy. Concentration camp survivor Ernst Bornstein wrote,

> One could identify *Muselmanner* by their physical and psychological decline; they were lethargic, indifferent to their surroundings, and could not stand up for more than a short period of time. Most other prisoners avoided contact with *Muselmanner*, in fear of contracting the condition themselves. The Nazis running the camps considered the *Muselmanner* undesirable, because they could not work or endure camp rule. Thus, during selections, these victims were the first to be sentenced to death. A person at the *Muselmann* stage had no chance for survival; he or she would not live for more than a few days or weeks.[33]

The nonbinary character of life and death is also exemplified by the treatment accorded to some of the inmates of contemporary Chinese prisons. Human rights groups have accused the Chinese government of harvesting the organs of condemned prisoners just before their executions—a practice designed to ensure the viability of the organs. The decedents are then thrown into mass graves, and all records of their lives and deaths erased.[34] These prisoners had already disappeared from life and needed only a short step forward to enter the kingdom of death. Their harvested organs, however, live on.

The Enemy Dead

In ancient Greece, the general presumption was that the bodies of fallen warriors, foes as well as friends, should be treated with honor. This idea is the key element of Sophocles' tragedy *Antigone*. Creon, the king of Thebes, refuses to allow the burial of Polynices, a rebel who led an invading foreign army against Creon. Despite Polynices' treachery, Creon is viewed as having violated an important religious precept. The gods subsequently punish the king by bringing a devastating plague to the city.

Today, most nations reject the Greek perspective and make an enormous distinction between their own dead and those of their foes. Among the most favored of the dead are a nation's soldiers who are killed in combat while fighting for their country. The U.S. military, like those of a number of other nations, makes every effort to recover the bodies of soldiers, sailors, and fliers killed in action so that they can be buried with honors in military cemeteries at home or abroad or at sea, if necessary. Those killed in naval battles were traditionally buried at sea with military honors, though today the ability to refrigerate and preserve remains on board ships sometimes makes this unnecessary.

The U.S. military has developed a very elaborate recovery system designed to retrieve and identify those killed in action whether in current battles, recent wars, or military engagements fought many decades in the past. This system was initiated after the Civil War when Union forces exhumed dead bodies from the battlefield graves where they had been left and transferred them to national military cemeteries where they were buried with military honors. Nearly three hundred thousand deceased Union soldiers were located and buried in seventy-five military cemeteries.[35]

In subsequent wars, U.S. commanders assigned such great importance to recovering the bodies of troops killed in combat that recovery units placed themselves at great risk from enemy fire to retrieve the bodies of fallen soldiers while battles raged around them. Occasionally, members of recovery teams are killed, necessitating the recovery of their bodies.[36] Long after the end of a war, the U.S. military will make extraordinary efforts to find and reclaim the bodies of deceased servicemen and servicewomen. Of course, this concern for recovery of the military dead is not limited to the United States. Israel, for example, has several times exchanged military or terrorist prisoners in its custody for the remains of deceased Israeli soldiers. In one case, Israel released two Syrian prisoners in exchange for the remains of an Israeli soldier killed thirty-seven years earlier.[37]

The remains of U.S. dead are generally prepared for return to the United States where they may be claimed by family members for private burials or interred in one of America's military cemeteries. Military funerals are designed to demonstrate the nation's gratitude and respect for the deceased warrior. In a solemn ceremony, before a flag-draped coffin, an honor guard salutes the soldier and family, "Taps" is sounded, and the burial flag properly folded and presented to the family. On national holidays, military cemeteries are festooned with flags, and family members come to pay respects to their deceased relatives. On Memorial Day, the president often lays a wreath at the Tomb of the Unknown Soldier at Arlington National Cemetery to honor those who lost their lives in the service of the United States.

Improper treatment of the military dead can lead to public revulsion as occurred recently when the press discovered that a benighted bureaucrat had consigned the remains of several hundred U.S. soldiers killed in Iraq to an unmarked grave. The Merit Systems

Protection Board castigated the hapless official for "reprehensible" and "appalling" conduct, and the news media gave the story prominent coverage.[38]

Against this backdrop of the honor and respect the United States shows its own military dead, the treatment accorded to enemy dead is especially glaring. Officially, the policy of the United States is to treat enemy dead with the same dignity as America's own fallen warriors. Under military law, mistreatment of enemy dead is a serious offense, subject to severe penalties. The reality, however, can be quite different.

One veteran of World War II wrote that some U.S. soldiers in the Pacific, "boiled the flesh off enemy skulls to make table ornaments for sweethearts or carved their bones into letter openers."[39] Acts of desecration were commonplace, with teeth and ears sliced off as souvenirs. Japanese dead were seldom buried but were stacked in piles and shoved by bulldozers into mass graves. The same was true during the Korean War when the bodies of Chinese and North Korean troops were often dragged into mass graves and buried without ceremony. Similar stories have emerged about U.S. conduct during the Gulf War.

Of course, not all enemies of the state are foreign soldiers. The Nazis murdered millions of Jews they deemed to be racial enemies, cremated the bodies, and buried them in unmarked mass graves. The Soviets and Chinese Communists murdered millions of individuals they regarded as political threats who were, likewise, thrown into mass graves and forgotten. Today, as we noted above, the Chinese government maintains prisons where political dissidents are transformed into *Muselmanner* before they are sent to oblivion. Take the case of Jintao Liu, a member of the outlawed Falun Gong movement who died in a Chinese prison before his story found its way into the Western press.

> Jintao Liu's body shuddered in pain as he endured yet another day of extreme torture.
>
> He had woken to pins being pushed into his nails before he was forced to stand still in a yard for some 18 hours. If he moved, he was beaten viciously and within an inch of his life.

Each excruciating second of the gruelling punishment caused his legs to swell as his body threatened to buckle under the pressure. He was given "no toilet breaks" and shown no mercy. Time had become his enemy—but not his worst.

That was a typical day for Liu during a lengthy stint in a series of Beijing detention centres and labour camps between 2006 and 2009.

There, he was subjected to electric shocks, medical tests, forced feedings, beatings, violent sexual assaults and other barbaric forms of torture designed by prison guards to humiliate and inflict maximum pain.[40]

Jintao Liu had entered the ranks of the *Muselmanner*—dead even before having to be buried.

Does the Treatment of the Dead Matter?

A long-standing philosophical and literary tradition holds that the body has no postmortem importance. James Joyce declared that a corpse was merely meat gone bad. Yet in most cultures the treatment of remains is conceived to be important, and there are a number of reasons why this is the case.

First, while the dead may have no interest in the treatment of their remains, the living often have a premortem concern with the matter. For whatever reason, people often leave detailed instructions in their wills concerning the disposition of their remains: they choose grave sites, write inscriptions, even direct that their remains be shot from cannons.

Second, remains are often important to family members and the community at large. As we saw, it is those without families or lacking ties to the community who receive anonymous burials in unmarked graves. For most families, a funeral and burial are important elements of the process of mourning a loved one. Respect for the body is an element of posthumous respect for the person. St. Augustine wrote that caring for the dead is a sign of piety, love, and affection and a source of comfort for the living.[41]

Third, governments promise immortality to loyal citizens through membership in the nation. The treatment of the worthy dead is a tangible symbol of this promise. Important leaders are entombed in mausoleums to symbolize their continuing fame. The most loyal of the dead, members of the military, are buried with special honors. Citizens in good standing find places in well-kept cemeteries and memorial gardens where their names are typically carved in stone. However, those who are not respectable members of the community—paupers, prison inmates, psychiatric patients—are unceremoniously consigned to anonymous graves and forgotten far from the bosom of the immortal nation. The corpses and graves of enemy dead are sometimes desecrated for good measure, clarifying their ineligibility for secular immortality.

Of course, in the end, memory is short and secular immortality is fleeting. Nearly everyone is eventually forgotten, most in one or two generations, some longer; a select few are remembered for centuries or even millennia eventually as phantasms and legends. But perhaps, life is preserved from oblivion when each generation remembers the previous one in an eternal chain. Or, perhaps, genetic continuity can serve as a form of immortality. The Hebrew prayer *l'dor v'dor*, from generation to generation, captures this idea. And, ironically, the Nazis seemed to agree when they declared their intention to erase all genetic trace of the Jews. Our genetic link to long-departed ancestors may be tenuous, but millions cling to this symbol of immortality when they pore through the charts and information sold to them by the burgeoning genealogy industry. The church required a lifetime of penitence, prayer, and charity for any hope of immortality, but today the whisper, at least, of genealogical immortality can be purchased for a few dollars.[42]

CHAPTER 6

Resurrection

T he dead, occasionally even those consigned to oblivion, retain some chance of resurrection. The idea of resurrection is usually understood in religious or supernatural terms. The resurrection of Jesus is, of course, a cornerstone of the Christian faith. In works of fiction, zombies, vampires, and other magically reanimated corpses rise from their tombs to wreak havoc among the living. Resurrection of the dead, though, can also be understood as a political phenomenon. Governments and contending political forces sometimes figuratively resurrect dead heroes or even armies of the dead to do battle for them. Some claim that science will eventually make actual resurrections possible. And, of course, millions of ordinary Americans seek to find meaning in their own lives by subscribing to such services as Ancestry.com to help them identify and animate long-dead ancestors who, they hope, will teach and inspire them.[1]

The idea of resurrecting the dead, whether in corporeal or spiritual form, has a long history. Many of the religions of the ancient world included concepts of reincarnation or resurrection in their belief systems. Though the two ideas overlap, believers generally view reincarnation as part of the natural cycle of life. After death, the soul or spirit of the decedent moves on and may eventually be reanimated in some new form, albeit generally retaining no memory of any prior corporeal existence. Resurrection, on the other hand, is a process through which the actual body or spirit of a decedent is brought back from the dead with memories it can express or that supposedly can be interpreted by the resurrector. Resurrection is not a natural process. It requires purposive action by a potent entity, perhaps a deity, powerful shaman, or necromancer, so the question of motivation, which is not an issue in reincarnation, is important in understanding resurrection.

One frequent motive for resurrecting the dead is a search for knowledge of the future. The dead are often thought to possess such knowledge, though those who question them are not always happy with the answers they receive. In the Hebrew Bible, for example, King Saul commands a medium to resurrect the prophet Samuel. Saul is facing an important battle against the Philistines and is desperate for the deceased prophet's counsel. The medium is able to raise the spirit of Samuel who terrifies Saul with his words:

> Samuel said to Saul, "Why have you disturbed me by bringing me up?"
>
> "I am in great distress," Saul said. "The Philistines are fighting against me, and God has departed from me. He no longer answers me, either by prophets or by dreams. So I have called on you to tell me what to do."
>
> Samuel said, "Why do you consult me, now that the Lord has departed from you and become your enemy? The Lord has done what he predicted through me. The Lord has torn the kingdom out of your hands and given it to one of your neighbors—to David. Because you did not obey the Lord or carry out his fierce wrath against the Amalekites, the Lord has done this to you today. The Lord will deliver both Israel and you into the hands of the Philistines, and tomorrow you and your sons will be with me. The Lord will also give the army of Israel into the hands of the Philistines."

Immediately Saul fell full length on the ground, filled with fear because of Samuel's words.[2]

Prophecy from the grave also brings evil tidings in Lucan's famous epic poem *Pharsalia*, based upon the long civil war that led to the end of the Roman Republic. One of the major figures in the war was the general Pompey, who was first the ally, then the bitter rival of Julius Caesar. In the poem, prior to what would later be seen as the decisive Battle of Pharsalus, Pompey's son Sextus travels to Thessaly to seek the counsel of the powerful witch Erictho. Sextus addresses the witch, saying,

> You are the pride of Thessalian witches. You have the power to reveal to mankind its future, the power to change the course of events. Please tell me exactly what turn the hazard of war is going to take. I am not just a Roman plebeian—I am the son of Pompey . . . —and I shall either rule the world or inherit disaster. I am worried because my heart is struck with doubts.[3]

Erictho grants Sextus's wish and uses gruesome rituals to animate the corpse of a recent decedent and raise its spirit from Hades. The witch whips the corpse with a live snake and forces it to answer Sextus's questions. When it speaks, the ghastly entity predicts that Pompey will be defeated. "The dead are looking forward to welcoming your father and his family in a quiet retreat, and they are reserving a place for the House of Pompey in the brighter region of their kingdom."[4] Pompey is, as prophesied, subsequently defeated by Caesar's forces and assassinated when he flees to Egypt.

From the dead Achilles, Odysseus also learns a dark truth. Achilles tells Odysseus that the land of the dead is a grim place. Achilles would prefer to return to life as the most humble of persons than remain in Hades as the "lord of the lifeless dead. I'd rather slave on earth for another man—some dirt-poor tenant farmer who scrapes to keep alive—than rule down here over all the breathless dead."[5]

Not every message from the dead brings despair. Sometimes those who are resurrected are said to communicate joy, hope, and inspiration. A premier example is, of course, the resurrection of Jesus. In the Christian Bible, Jesus is resurrected on the third day after his crucifixion. According to the Gospel of Mark, Mary Magdalene and two other women arrive at Jesus's tomb and find it empty. The Gospel of Matthew avers that an angel then appeared to Mary Magdalene telling her that God has raised Jesus from the dead. Much later, the leaders of the new religion claimed that after his death Jesus appeared to other followers and even resurrected several recently deceased individuals, including Paul, before ascending to heaven. Unlike Samuel or the shade summoned by Erictho who brought unwelcome tidings to their interlocutors, Jesus brought what his followers called "the good news" that the faithful would be saved and would themselves be resurrected at Christ's second coming.

Both Saul and Sextus relied on magic to resurrect the dead, but their purpose was mundane, not metaphysical. They did not hope to acquire some arcane bit of lore; rather they pursued the real-world purpose of learning the outcome of impending battles. The idea of Jesus's resurrection also had mundane aspects. For the first several decades after Jesus's death, his resurrection was understood in spiritual terms, that is, his spirt ascended to heaven. This claim was not a particularly remarkable one. The spirit of any righteous person might have been said to have followed this path.

The idea that Jesus had been physically resurrected as well as his promise of eventual resurrection for the faithful (the good news) is first mentioned in the Gospel of Mark, written some four decades after the events it describes. During these four decades, Jerusalem had been destroyed in the Jewish-Roman War; Jews were killed, sent into exile, or enslaved; and the tiny group of Jews who followed Jesus's disciples was in danger of disappearing along with many other small Jewish apocalyptic splinter groups.[6]

The claim that he had been physically resurrected distinguished Jesus's followers from all the others.[7] This claim was attractive to adherents of pagan beliefs and various cults of the period. Traditional Greek and Roman religions, for example, reserved the possibility of physical resurrection for great heroes like Achilles, Heracles, and Memnon, while ordinary individuals could only hope for a shadowy postmortem existence as disembodied souls. Early Christian leaders calculated that the promise of general physical resurrection would fulfill a longing among pagans for the reward that had previously been available only to heroes and, thus, inspire flocks of converts.[8] The new creed did not have much success among Jews, for whom physical resurrection was not an important or widely held belief, but did prove appealing to adherents of pagan religions who were already familiar with the concept.

Legal Resurrection of the Dead in Court

Today, the dead are most often resurrected in the courtroom. Under some circumstances, their testimony can be presented. When the dead are unable to speak for themselves, forensic scientists can speak for them. The testimony of the dead is heard in criminal cases under the so-called "dying declaration" exception to the "hearsay rule." The hearsay rule generally bars the admission of testimony that quotes persons who are not present in court for cross-examination. Thus, a claim by one person that he or she heard some absent third party admit to a crime is not admissible.

The dying declaration is one of the major exceptions to the hearsay rule. The statement of a decedent—who obviously cannot be present in court—is allowed into evidence when the statement concerns the cause of the individual's death and the declarant believed their death was imminent and inevitable.[9] This exception can be traced to a 1789 English case, *The King v. Woodcock*.[10] The judge in the case admitted into evidence a dying statement from a woman who said her husband had caused her injuries by beating her. The judge justified admitting the deceased woman's statement on the grounds that such statements "are made in extremity, when the party is at the point of death, and when every hope of this world is gone: when every motive to falsehood is silenced, and the mind is induced by the most powerful considerations to speak the truth." This idea was echoed by the U.S. Supreme Court in the case of *Mattox v. U.S.* where the high court held that "the certain expectation of almost immediate death will remove all temptation to falsehood, and enforce as strict adherence to the truth as the obligation of an oath could impose."[11]

Courts have, nevertheless, raised questions about the reliability of dying declarations. Just a few years after the *Mattox* decision cited above, the U.S. Supreme Court observed that "a dying declaration by no means imports absolute verity. . . . The history of criminal trials is replete with instances where witnesses, even in the agonies of death, have through malice, misapprehension, or weakness of mind made declarations that were inconsistent with the actual facts."[12]

Such declarations, however, tend to sway juries. Western cultural and religious tradition ensures that a voice from the grave will speak with authority. In one case, Tonya Jones was arrested and tried for the murder of her husband, Donyea Jones. The chief witness against Tonya was her deceased husband. In a deathbed statement to the police, Donyea asserted that he had been murdered by his wife. "My wife poured gasoline on me and lit me on fire," Donyea said before he died.

Tonya's attorney challenged Donyea's testimony pointing out that his statement contained several inconsistencies. The attorney also suggested that Donyea had abused his wife and had harbored malice toward her, which might have raised doubts about the veracity of his accusation. The jury, however, accepted the truth of the now-dead Donyea's declaration. Tonya's attorney observed, "It was extremely difficult for these jurors to get past, 'Why would anybody say something like that if it weren't true?'"[13]

Forensic scientists collect and analyze evidence related to the commission of crimes. They appear in court to present and interpret the significance of the evidence. Forensic science includes a number of subspecialities: forensic pathologists specialize in conducting autopsies on recent decedents, forensic anthropologists study skeletal remains, forensic odontologists study bite marks, and so forth.

The origins of forensics can be traced to ancient China. In the thirteenth century, physician and scholar Song Ci published a manual offering guidance for the scientific solution of criminal cases. Song's manual offered advice on conduct of autopsies, the protection of evidence, and the determination of causes of death.[14] In the West, the emergence of forensic science was delayed by church prohibitions on the dissection of cadavers. Nevertheless, bodies were studied throughout the Middle Ages, and in 1533, Charles V of France decreed that courts make use of evidence from autopsies in cases of infanticide, homicide, and possible poisoning.[15] In the ensuing centuries, forensic science has become a dominant factor in criminal investigations.

Prior to the advent of forensic science, crimes were solved by inducing a guilty party to confess or by securing eyewitness testimony. Sometimes identifying the guilty party entailed little more than finding someone with a motive or enemies in the community. None of these modes of investigation is especially reliable. In the case of a homicide, forensics allows what amounts to a postmortem interview with the victim. Take the famous case of Ted Bundy, a serial killer accused of the brutal murders of a number of young women in Washington, Oregon, Utah, and Colorado during the 1970s. The key piece of evidence that led to Bundy's conviction and eventual electrocution was produced by forensic analysis. A forensic odontologist testified that his examination of several of the victims produced bite marks that were a match for Bundy's teeth. Several jurors told later interviewers that these bite marks were, in their minds, the crucial piece of evidence in the trial.[16] With the help of a forensic scientist, Bundy's victims had reached from the grave to identify him.

Today, DNA evidence has become the gold standard in criminal cases. In the case of a homicide, the victim's body will be carefully searched for foreign DNA, and matching DNA found on the victim with the DNA of a suspect seems sure proof of guilt. Occasionally, a jury will reject DNA evidence in favor of some alternative explanation of the crime. An example is the infamous 1995 murders of Nicole Brown Simpson and Ronald Goldman when, despite DNA evidence, the jury allowed itself to be convinced that Nicole Simpson's former husband, O. J. Simpson, was not guilty of the crime. Generally speaking, however, juries give a great deal of credence to forensic evidence, perhaps too much credence given the possibility of faulty interpretations.[17] The voice of the dead, amplified by science, carries a great deal of weight.

The Politics of Resurrection

Resurrection can play an important role in political affairs. Since ancient times, the dead have been viewed as possessing special power, and as a result, their words have always carried special weight.[18] Of course, since the dead are generally unable to speak for themselves, those who resurrect them usually deliver the message, interpret its meaning, and ultimately benefit from its power.

In ancient times, efforts to literally resurrect the dead involved complex and sometimes vile practices including the sacrifice of young boys and infants.[19] Today, efforts to raise the dead are generally figurative rather than literal and are more likely to involve historical research and exegesis than ritual sacrifice and hieroscopy. It may seem odd to compare historical research to necromancy, but historians, along with biographers, forensic scientists, newspaper writers, and others, endeavor to understand and speak for the views of the dead. Historians and biographers often claim to discover previously unknown facts about famous people or to identify (unearth) individuals whose ideas—even existence—had been unknown or forgotten. Such discoveries allow their authors to engage with the decedent and offer an interpretation or reinterpretation of his or her words and thoughts. For example, Dr. Paula Byrne, an expert on the life and work of Jane Austen, recently discovered a lost portrait of the famous novelist that suggested that the prevailing understanding of Austen and the meaning of her work was wrong. Byrne said, "This new picture, first roots [Austen] in a London setting—by Westminster Abbey. And second, it presents her as a professional woman writer; there are pens on the table, a sheaf of paper. She seems to be a woman very confident in her own skin, very happy to be presented as a professional woman writer and a novelist, which does fly in the face of the cutesy, heritage spinster view."[20] The newly discovered "real"

Austen seemed by no means to refute the older view of the author as an ideal Regency woman—timid and dependent.

Governments, as well as major social and political forces, make use of historical exegesis to figuratively resurrect the dead. Governments work to animate important historical figures who will promote national unity and popular consent by attesting to the virtues of the nation and its current political institutions. After Chairman Mao Zedong's death in 1976, China's leadership embalmed his body and placed it on display in a huge and ornate mausoleum where it lies in a crystal sarcophagus surrounded by flowers. Thousands of visitors file past the sarcophagus every day. Mao had fostered a personality cult during his lifetime, but his initial successors, particularly Deng Xiaoping, abandoned the cult of Mao that they thought interfered with China's modernization. Mao's "Cultural Revolution" was now denounced by party leaders as a time of chaos.

China's current leaders, however, believe that Mao's support, albeit posthumous, is an important instrument of national unity and promotes the legitimacy of the nation's contemporary leadership. Criticism of Mao's leadership is, once again, prohibited. China's leaders watched as the Soviet Union's rejection of its ideology and history and, particularly, abandonment of the veneration of Vladimir Lenin and Joseph Stalin helped to precipitate the regime's loss of legitimacy and collapse. Hence, in recent years, new statues of Mao have been erected, new portraits hung, and Mao's photo emblazoned upon Chinese currency. Mao's words are again pondered and praised. For example, President Xi Jinping ordered party leaders and cadres to study an obscure, seventy-year-old pamphlet authored by Mao titled *Work Method of Party Committees*, to help them enhance discipline and encourage harmony among comrades.[21] Tens of thousands of copies of the pamphlet were quickly printed and distributed. To legitimate his own leadership and strengthen his own personality cult, President Xi has evoked Maoist phraseology, encouraging the Chinese media to refer to him as a "helmsman" and "people's leader," terms once used by and about Mao.

While U.S. leaders' personality cults are generally not as extreme as those that have evolved in China and elsewhere in recent decades,

U.S. presidents and other significant persons are often figuratively resurrected to lend their support to current governments and to their programs. Abraham Lincoln is today among the most venerated of U.S. presidents, ranked by many as America's greatest leader. During his lifetime, however, opinion on Lincoln was rather mixed. Historian David Donald called Lincoln "wildly unpopular" in his own time." Lincoln received less than 40 percent of the popular presidential vote in 1860, and in 1864, even with the Southern states not participating in the election, 45 percent of the nation's remaining voters preferred Democratic candidate General George B. McClellan. Many of Lincoln's fellow Republicans frequently expressed contempt for him. Abolitionist leader Wendell Phillips called Lincoln "a huckster in politics" and "a first-rate second-rate man."[22] Some shed no tears at the news of the president's assassination. During the war, Lincoln was frequently denounced even by the Northern press. As the *New York Times* reported in May 1864,

> No living man was ever charged with political crimes of such multiplicity and such enormity as Abraham Lincoln. He has been denounced without end as a perjurer, a usurper, a tyrant, a subverter of the Constitution, a destroyer of the liberties of his country, a reckless desperado, a heartless trifler over the last agonies of an expiring nation. Had that which has been said of him been true there is no circle in Dante's Inferno full enough of torment to expiate his iniquities.[23]

And though Lincoln is remembered as a modern-day Moses who freed the slaves, his actual views on slavery were mixed. In his first inaugural address Lincoln supported the idea of a constitutional amendment that would protect the institution of slavery from federal interference and sometimes spoke favorably of the deportation of all Black people to their African lands of origin.

Not long after Lincoln's assassination, however, the sixteenth president was figuratively resurrected by the leaders of the Republican party who controlled the national government. Lincoln was presented as a demigod whose every word and deed merited praise and emulation. Secretary of War Edwin Stanton organized Lincoln's funeral, including a 1,600 mile procession in which a special train carried the late president's bloody corpse around the North, as a "massive propaganda tool" to support the Republican plan for "reconstruction" of the South. Republican leaders sought to remind Northern voters of the sacrifice President Lincoln and his Republican party had made to save the Union. Stanton "made the martyr's corpse a traveling exhibit of Southern wickedness."[24] This funeral procession marked the beginning of the "bloody shirt" campaigns waged by Republicans against their Democratic foes for the next several decades. Ministers compared Lincoln and his death to Jesus and the crucifixion. Republican presidents claimed Lincoln's endorsement and his support for their policies. Surely, it was said, Lincoln would have favored high tariffs, urged annexation of the Philippines, opposed socialism, populism, and labor unions, and endorsed whatever programs Republican leaders promoted. Eventually, even Democrats claimed Lincoln's blessing.

Over the next several decades, Lincoln's words and speeches, which had often been ignored or greeted with derision even by the Republican press, were republished, taught in the schools, and even read in churches as though they were drawn from the holy scripture. Lincoln's brief remarks at the November 19, 1863, consecration of the national cemetery at Gettysburg, Pennsylvania, were generally overlooked by the press or, in the case of Democratic newspapers like the *Chicago Tribune*, dismissed as "silly, flat and dishwatery."[25] Lincoln was not the principal speaker that day—the main address was given by Congressman Edward Everett of Massachusetts—and the audience seemed unimpressed by Lincoln's remarks. Historian Shelby Foote wrote that after Lincoln's presentation the applause was scattered and "barely polite."[26] Lincoln's Gettysburg speech was soon forgotten.[27] Indeed, in the immediate aftermath of the war, it was the president's Emancipation Proclamation announcing an end to slavery that was most frequently quoted, particularly in the Republican press.

The Gettysburg Address was given new life in the closing years of the nineteenth century. By the 1880s Reconstruction had ended, and

Northern sympathy for the slaves freed by the Emancipation Proclamation had waned after years of unflattering newspaper accounts of
the South's Reconstruction-era Black politicians. Northerners were
more inclined to empathize with white Southerners for the hardships
they had suffered during and after the war. Indeed, the version of
history associated with the Dunning school and popularized by such
films as *Birth of a Nation* would soon persuade Northern Whites that
freed Blacks were ignorant and savage, incapable of self-government,
and hardly deserving of sympathy. Gradually, the once-celebrated
Emancipation Proclamation faded from public discourse, except
in the Black community. In its place, official and popular attention
turned to Lincoln's Gettysburg Address.

Since Lincoln had only been figuratively resurrected and was
not available to interpret his words, Republican and then Democratic politicians began citing the address as evidence of Lincoln's
support for national unity and patriotism and for their own political
principles. In the address, Lincoln had not mentioned slavery but
had spoken of a war to save the Union and its Republican form
of government. During the late nineteenth-century era of national
reconciliation, Lincoln's words were interpreted as applying equally
to both Union and Confederate soldiers. All had "given their
lives' for the nation. Later, leaders of the Progressive movement,
including Presidents Theodore Roosevelt and William Howard
Taft, interpreted Lincoln's phrase "all men are created equal" not
to refer to slavery but, instead, to indicate Lincoln's endorsement
for the political reforms favored by Progressives. Still later, New
Dealers asserted that these same words demonstrated Lincoln's
opposition to economic inequality.[28]

The Gettysburg Address, in its entirety, is carved in the interior
wall of the Lincoln Memorial in Washington, D.C., completed in
1922. This magnificent shrine is visited by thousands of Americans
every year. Here, they can be inspired by Lincoln's message of
national unity and endorsement of the idea that today's Americans
should dedicate themselves to the furtherance of America's special
and still unfinished work. Lincoln wrote,

It is for us the living, rather, to be dedicated here to the unfinished work which they who fought here have thus far so nobly advanced. It is rather for us to be here dedicated to the great task remaining before us—that from these honored dead we take increased devotion to that cause for which they here gave the last full measure of devotion—that we here highly resolve that these dead shall not have died in vain—that this nation, under God, shall have a new birth of freedom—and that government of the people, by the people, for the people, shall not perish from the earth.[29]

In this way, a president whom many disdained in life continues to be a powerful figure in death.

Narratives and Counternarratives

Lincoln, like Mao, was figuratively resurrected by a victorious political party and, like Mao, has been maintained as a focus of respect and adulation by a government that sees him as an important symbol of national pride and unity. But, just as governments resurrect their heroes, political and social dissidents reach into their own histories to identify sometimes forgotten, often long-dead individuals whose ideas and actions might inspire others to join their cause. In some instances, too, dissidents endeavor to discredit their opponents' heroes and send them back to oblivion.

In contemporary America, groups like Black Lives Matter (BLM) seek to sanctify Black persons like the late George Floyd, killed by the police, to resurrect African Americans long ignored by mainstream (white) historians, and to vilify time-honored American heroes, especially those of the Confederacy, literally knocking them from their pedestals. The resurrection of forgotten African Americans was precisely the point of a volume edited by Ibram X. Kendi and Keisha N. Blain titled *Four Hundred Souls*.[30] The purpose of this resurrection of the dead is to inspire the living with a sense of community and common purpose. The resurrected dead in this volume, speaking through Kendi, Blain, and other historians, collectively attempt to correct a historical record that, they say, has been falsified, particularly since Reconstruction.

During the late nineteenth and early twentieth centuries most histories of Reconstruction emphasized the suffering and struggles of Southern whites in the wake of the Civil War. This historical perspective sympathetic to Southern whites was presented in such works as the famous 1940 film *Gone With the Wind*, as well as by D. W. Griffith's enormously popular 1915 silent-screen epic, *Birth of a Nation*, which ends with the heroic knights of the Ku Klux Klan riding to the rescue of a group of innocent whites besieged by a band of former slaves, depicted as savages intent upon rape and murder. This latter film debuted in a special White House screening where it was received with great enthusiasm by President Woodrow Wilson. Wilson reportedly remarked, "It is like writing history with lightning, and my only regret is that it is all so terribly true."[31] When the film was shown to popular audiences it sparked a number of attacks by whites upon Blacks throughout the nation. Pre–World War II academic history and school texts, dominated by the so-called Dunning school, emphasized the unreadiness or incapacity of newly freed Blacks to exercise political rights, excoriated Northern Radical Republicans for imposing "Negro rule" upon the prostrate South, and applauded the efforts of white Southerners to reclaim their rightful political supremacy in the region.[32] The Dunning school was named for turn-of-the-twentieth century Columbia University history professor William Dunning. He and his followers sympathized with Southern whites and believed that granting newly freed Blacks the right to vote and hold office had been a major error.

Beginning in the 1950s and 1960s, this version of U.S. history began to be inconsistent with changing conceptions of race relations and with a liberal democratic political agenda calling for Black voting rights and greater racial equality. Accordingly, the older historical narrative came under attack as blatantly racist and inaccurate. By the 1970s, the history of Reconstruction was being rewritten to emphasize the injustices visited upon Blacks by Southern whites in the aftermath of the Civil War. Rather than watch *Birth of a Nation*, tens of millions of Americans viewed *Roots*, a 1977 ABC television miniseries that depicted with great sympathy the plight of African Americans during slavery and Reconstruction. Most of the whites portrayed in this film were villainous, and it was the turn of the Ku Kluxers to be depicted as murderous brutes. And, for their part, academic historians made it their business to rewrite the official history of Reconstruction to emphasize the accomplishments of African Americans in the realm of politics and government until their abandonment by Northern politicians and suppression by white Southerners. Even in the South, this is the history generally learned by schoolchildren today. As historian Eric Foner has noted, the old history of Reconstruction reflected and was designed to reinforce one set of political understandings, while the revised history was intended to comport with and reinforce contemporary understandings born during the civil rights era.[33]

In recent years, African American scholars and activists have taken matters a step further. Nikole Hannah-Jones and other authors associated with the "1619 Project," for example, worked to place the institution of slavery at the center of U.S. history as well as to point to the major and unrecognized contribution made by enslaved persons and their descendants to the growth of the U.S. economy and American power in the world.[34] To this end, Hannah-Jones figuratively resurrected the four hundred thousand unremembered enslaved Africans transported to the American colonies. The first group, according to Hannah-Jones, included a man named Anthony and a woman named Isabella, brought to North America on a slave ship in 1619.

Hannah-Jones goes on to speak for these anonymous enslaved Black persons and their descendants who were ignored when they lived, consigned to isolated slave cemeteries when they died, and then forgotten as they helped build the United States. They cleared land, taught white colonists to grow rice and inoculate themselves against smallpox, and grew cotton—America's most important export. By resurrecting the dead, Hannah-Jones shows that many of America's traditional heroes were complicit in and deserving of censure for their roles in the evil of slavery. For example, as Thomas Jefferson sat composing the ringing words of the Declaration of Independence, which declared that all men are created equal, he was attended by an enslaved Black teenage boy, Robert Hemings. The fourteen-year-old Hemings was the son of Elizabeth Hemings, an enslaved woman, and John Wayles, Jefferson's father-in-law. Hemings served as Jefferson's valet.

The dead speak with great power. Their authority lends weight to arguments for Black political solidarity, a rethinking of U.S. race relations, and perhaps, the payment of reparations to the descendants of slaves and Black victims of racial injustice. The latter is one of Hannah-Jones's major points. Black intellectuals have long claimed that reparations were due. But it was not until the power of the dead was brought to bear on its behalf that the idea of reparations began to gain traction, with some communities, like Evanston, Illinois, announcing plans to actually provide reparations to its Black citizens.

The Holocaust

Another case of resurrecting the dead to inspire solidarity and pride among the living is the Holocaust, or *shoah* as it is known in Hebrew. After the Likud bloc came to power in Israel during the mid-1970s, and especially after the 1983 Israeli invasion of Lebanon and the continuing occupation and settlement of the West Bank by Israelis, Jewish organizations began to feel that U.S. Jewish support for Israel had weakened. Their response was to de-emphasize support for Israel—which had been the major focus in their efforts to maintain Jewish solidarity—and turn to other rallying points. Support for Israel has, of course, never been abandoned. However, many left-liberal American Jews have become critical of Israeli policy, and some have begun to participate in the "anti-Zionist" discourse that has become prominent on the political Left. To avoid alienating liberal Jews who oppose the policies of conservative Israeli administrations, some Jewish organizations have sought to develop other, less "controversial," mobilizing themes. The most important of these has been remembrance of the Holocaust.[35]

Through the 1960s and 1970s, the annual United Jewish Appeal Spring fund-raising drive, conducted through direct solicitations and telethons in every Jewish community in the nation, had focused mainly on the need to help Israel. Solicitation letters and calls emphasized Israel's military needs, housing needs, desert reclamation, children's programs, and so forth. By the 1980s and 1990s, faced with some unease among more liberal American Jews about Israel's right-wing political leadership and treatment of Arabs, the annual campaign moved toward a policy of reduced emphasis on Israel and greater emphasis on other issues. Most important among these was the Holocaust. During the actual Holocaust, American Jewish organizations, politicians, and high-ranking Jewish government officials had been shamefully silent, more concerned with anti-Semitism at home than with the fate of millions of Jews in Europe.[36]

Indeed, when Joseph Proskauer became president of the American Jewish Committee (AJC) in 1943, his acceptance speech, which dealt with the problems American Jews were likely to face in the postwar period, made no mention whatsoever of the ongoing slaughter of European Jews or of any possible rescue efforts.[37] Similarly, the "Statement of Views," adopted by the AJC's 1943 annual meeting has no mention of the Germans' ongoing efforts to destroy the European Jews, something that was already known by all American Jewish leaders at that time.[38]

In the years following World War II, moreover, Jewish organizations for the most part ignored the Holocaust, and the few Holocaust survivors to reach the United States were typically led to understand that they should remain silent about their experiences. I can personally recall that when my parents and I arrived in the United States, after several years in a displaced persons camp, our relatives cautioned my parents not to talk about their experiences during the war. "Nobody wants to hear about those things," said one cousin.

American Jewish leaders were embarrassed about the cowardice they themselves had shown, eager to avoid charges of inaction, and never anxious to link themselves in any way to the benighted Jews of Europe. One source of shame, of course, was the apparent absence of Jewish resistance to the Germans. American Jews often felt contempt for their European brethren who, the Americans thought, had "allowed" themselves to be killed. The Americans resented being associated with people who seemed not only to confirm but to give new meaning to the stereotype of Jewish timidity. Jews, it appeared, had been too spineless to fight even when being herded toward the gas chambers.[39] The truth, of course, was that Jews had fought bravely in many ways, especially through their service in the Soviet army.[40] This fact, however, was hardly likely to be embraced by American Jews during the 1950s.

During the 1970s, however, a new generation of Jewish leaders emerged who had no complicity in the events of the war years and who could, indeed, use their inaction during the Holocaust to discredit and displace the established leaders of the Jewish community. The story of the Holocaust, moreover, became a useful parable on the dangers of assimilation and the evil of which even the best Gentiles were capable. After all, had not the Jews lived in Germany for centuries? Did many German Jews not regard themselves as Germans first and Jews second? Did their German friends and neighbors not turn on the Jews in a murderous rage?

During the 1970s, this version of the story of the Holocaust began to join or even to replace Bible stories as mechanisms through which to teach American Jews—especially American Jewish children—to be wary of identifying too closely with the world of Gentile America. American Jews might think of themselves as Americans, but did not the German Jews think they were Germans before being reminded of their true identity? One history of the Holocaust written for American Jewish children points out that even "Jews who did not consider themselves to be Jews were sought out by the Nazis and forced to wear the badge. Some startled Christians found they had

Jewish blood from some grandfather or grandmother. They also had to wear the star."[41]

As Jewish organizations began to make the Holocaust an increasingly central focus of their organizational and fund-raising activities, Holocaust survivors were honored rather than told to be quiet; Holocaust studies became a major focus of activity for the young; and Holocaust memorials, museums, and commemorations became central parts of the agenda of all Jewish institutions. The Holocaust even entered the Jewish liturgy as a special day of prayer and remembrance, Yom Hashoah, was added to the religious calendar by Conservative and Reform, though usually not by the most Orthodox, synagogues.

Rare today is the fund-raising appeal from a Jewish organization that does not remind the potential donor of the Holocaust and of contemporary efforts by neo-Nazi "revisionists" to claim that the Holocaust never took place—efforts that, it is said, must be countered by cash contributions. Rather than feel shame over the alleged lack of Jewish resistance to the Germans, American Jewish organizations now celebrate the Warsaw ghetto uprising, which is said to have held the Germans at bay longer than the entire Polish army had been able to do in 1939.

One popular history of the Holocaust, used in Jewish schools throughout the United States, is subtitled, "A History of Courage and Resistance."[42] Of its twenty-two chapters, nearly half focus on themes of Jewish defiance and heroism. Chapter titles include "A Leader in the Underground," "Women Fighters," and "The Doctor Warriors." A young student reading this or one of several similar texts might easily conclude that everywhere in Europe ragtag bands of Jewish partisans fought the *Wehrmacht* to a standstill. Two full chapters recount the tale of the Warsaw ghetto uprising, concluding with the obligatory observation that "the Jews in the ghetto with their pitiable weapons, held out longer against their Nazi enemies than the Poles had held out when the Germans attacked Poland." As I have shown elsewhere, the Jews did play an important role in the defeat of Nazi Germany, as weapons engineers, cryptanalysts, and soldiers in the

Soviet and U.S. armies, but historical accuracy does not seem to be relevant in this context.[43]

The prominence currently given to the story of the Warsaw ghetto tragedy is especially ironic given the lack of a response among American Jewish leaders to the uprising when it actually occurred. In April and May 1943, as the ghetto was being liquidated by the Germans, Jewish resistance fighters made a series of dramatic broadcasts and desperate calls for help over their clandestine radio station. On April 22, the station broadcast, "Gun salvos are echoing in Warsaw's streets. Women and children are defending themselves with bare hands. Come to our aid!" On May 25, the BBC reported monitoring a broadcast telling of Jews being executed by firing squads and by being burned alive. Yet many American Jewish organizations had other priorities during this period and gave little attention to the grim news from Warsaw.[44] Today, however, resurrecting these dead serves the purposes of the living. Indeed, after their resurrection the silenced voices of millions of murdered Jews spoke with more power than they had exercised in their former lives.

Is Actual Resurrection Possible?

The dead can be resurrected figuratively, but can they be resurrected physically? A number of scientists and futurists say they can. Proposed methods include cryonics, digital reconstruction of individual personalities, recreation by powerful AIs, and a variety of other techniques.[45] All these ideas are speculative and largely based upon yet-to-be-developed technologies. But, of course, yesterday's science fiction is today's science.

Writers in this realm make the assumption that most individuals would choose to be brought back from the dead if it was possible. This is a rather questionable assumption. Some of the dead might wish to return, some not. Nearly fifty thousand Americans kill themselves every year. Whatever the reason, they have chosen death. Should it be up to the living to overrule and reverse that decision?

Of course, the living do just this every day by making heroic efforts to resuscitate those who attempt suicide, but the ethical propriety of such efforts is open to question.[46]

Some faiths consider necromancy a sin. And in literature as well as some religious traditions, the dead usually do not wish to return. The corpse resurrected by Erictho had to be tortured to induce it to speak. Presumably Walter Benjamin might have faced torture too, if he had been resurrected by the *Gestapo*. Besides, most Americans are convinced that the resurrected dead would be angry and feral: witness the popularity of zombie films. Who can say they are wrong.

Death and Change

ome 2,500 years ago, Socrates said that the central purpose of philosophy was to teach individuals to prepare themselves for the moment of dying and the state of death.[1] If Socrates was correct, philosophy has been a rather dismal failure. Most persons fear death and would do much to forestall their own demise. "Of all the things that move man," wrote cultural anthropologist Ernest Becker, "one of the principal ones is his terror of death."[2]

This terror manifests itself in a variety of ways. One is hero worship. Many individuals look to heroic leaders to protect them from death. Heroes, in turn, demonstrate this mastery by wielding death against their foes. Another common manifestation of concern about dying is the widespread obsession with physical fitness and the maintenance of a youthful appearance.[3] And, of course, the fear of death and hope for some form of immortality are a source of power for religions, political movements, and governments. In his well-known work *On the Nature of Things*, the Roman philosopher Lucretius wrote that it was their fear of death that made humans feel a sense of dependence on both religious and secular authorities.[4]

The success of the Christian religion, as we saw, resulted in large measure from the claim that Jesus had returned from the grave and would bring about the resurrection of his followers. This claim allowed Christianity to compete successfully with various cults of the time that also featured healers with supernatural powers who had risen from the dead. The joyful Easter shout, "Christ has risen!" echoed the ceremonies practiced by these cults.[5] As to states, not only do they offer ersatz afterlives, but they deconstruct death and work to defeat it in detail, depriving the Grim Reaper of some of its most powerful weapons.

Some futurists, though, say that death could be confronted more directly and, if not eliminated, at least delayed for centuries or even millennia.[6] One popular idea among self-styled futurists is mind-to-computer uploading, which would entail transferring the human consciousness into a computer system. A less ambitious version of this concept is the transformation of humans into cyborgs that while not immortal, might live for centuries. Other futurists look to cloning, genetic engineering, regenerative medicine, and nanotechnology for indefinite extensions of the human life span. These claims are, to be sure, speculative and depend upon the development of technologies that do not yet exist in such fields as cybernetics and robotics. One scientific skeptic responded sarcastically to an article about the imminence of a solution to the problem of ageing by declaring that futurists should join him in an effort "to solve another engineering challenge, one that had been too long ignored by the ultra-conservative, fraidy-cat mainstream scientific community: the problem of producing flying pigs."[7]

Immortality was once a gift or curse from the gods. But what of secular immortality? Even if possible, would a world without death be desirable? Perhaps not. Though it holds terror for individuals, death is a great, and perhaps necessary, engine of societal change. Consider three problems: immortal but malevolent rulers, cognitive entrenchment, and new forms of society.

Immortal but Malevolent Rulers

Over time, many of the world's leaders have been malevolent—concerned only with their own interests, willing to brutalize their subjects, and all too ready to attack their neighbors.[8] In modern times, the names Hitler, Stalin, and Mao are synonymous with murder and terror. Unfortunately, political power seems to attract individuals who suffer from narcissistic personality disorders. The political philosopher Thomas Hobbes said, "A restless desire for power is in all men . . . a perpetual and restless desire of power after power, that ceaseth only in death."[9] To be sure, individuals vary in the extent to which they are affected by Hobbes's "restless desire." Some seem content to lead quiet lives in which they command nothing more challenging than their television tuners. Others, however, appear to perpetually strive for important offices and positions that place them in charge of people, resources, and significant policy decisions.

In the United States every year, thousands of individuals compete for local, state, and national political office. Some seem driven to constantly strive for higher and higher office, seemingly equating the desirability of the position with the power its occupant commands. Local politicians seek opportunities to run for state office, state-level politicians constantly eye national offices, and national politicians often harbor presidential ambitions. A number of well-known U.S. politicians invested years, or even decades, seeking election to the presidency. Politicians like Al Gore, John Kerry, and Hillary Rodham Clinton (and in an earlier era Henry Clay) devoted large fractions of their lives to unsuccessful presidential quests. Others, like Richard Nixon, Bill Clinton, and Barack Obama struggled for years and finally succeeded. One recent president, Donald Trump, was reluctant to concede his defeat at the polls, claimed he had been cheated, and at least tacitly encouraged his supporters to storm the Capitol so that he might remain in the White House.

What drives such individuals to commit themselves to lives of meetings, official dinners, and deals, a life of fund-raising and negotiation, a life of media scrutiny? According to presidential scholar Richard Shenkman, these aspirants for high office are "frighteningly overambitious, willing to sacrifice their health, family, loyalty and values as they sought to overcome the obstacles to power."[10] The modern presidential selection system, which virtually requires aspirants to devote years to a single-minded quest for office, probably selects for an extraordinary level of ambition and, perhaps, ruthlessness among the major contenders for office.[11] One long-time member of Congress told me that he had served through several presidencies and had become concerned that every recent occupant of the White House was, in his words, a "monster." They had, in essence, succumbed to Hobbes's perpetual desire for power.

In democracies, perhaps, monstrous leaders can be voted out of office. Few of the world's 165 independent nations, however, are fully democratic—only twenty-three according to a recent *Economist* survey.[12] And even in the democracies, as we saw in the United States in 2021, some leaders may not willingly leave office. In much of the world, particularly monstrous leaders leave office only when they die—whether from natural causes or, often enough, by assassination. As Jones and Olken observe in a recent paper, between 1875 and 2004, fifty-nine national leaders, mainly autocrats, were assassinated. Usually, these assassinations produced beneficial effects for the nations in question.[13] Then, consider a world without death. Would the world's most ruthless autocrats—the Hitlers, Stalins, and Maos—rule for all eternity? Futurists who long for a world without death might consider this question.

Cognitive Entrenchment

A second question is the potential impact of immortality on innovation and creativity. Since no immortals exist, we cannot measure their levels of creativity. A great deal of work has, however, been done on the impact of ageing on intellectual ability and creativity. Ageing is not necessarily associated with senescence. It is, however, linked to a gradual decline in creativity and innovative capacity.

One often used measure of the impact of age on creativity is the sheer number of new works produced by scientists, authors, and artists over their lifetimes. The publication of scientific work or production of artistic work requires creative effort, and both scientific and artistic productivity, as measured by the absolute number of works produced, tends, over time, to resemble an inverted U, with the production of new work rising during individuals' twenties and thirties, then declining from age forty onward. After age sixty, the productivity of scientists decreases sharply and that of artists, musicians, and writers even more sharply.[14] Both groups seem less able to create new work.

Some students of intellectual creativity distinguish between *experimental innovators* and *conceptual innovators*.[15] Experimental innovators are those who work on a problem for long periods of time and develop new methods or processes based upon extended observation and incremental advances. Conceptual innovators, on the other hand, are those who make sudden, radical, unexpected leaps that in a flash of insight, change accepted understandings and ways of doing things. Albert Einstein is, of course, the premier example.

Experimental innovators may continue to work as they age, and often, their production of important work peaks when they are in their fifties, sixties, or even seventies. Experimental innovators work gradually, and their discoveries emerge incrementally over the course of their careers. Conceptual innovators are more likely to depend upon intuition and insight than experimentation and observation. Conceptual innovators often have little commitment to established ideas and ways of thinking and tend to be younger people.

Older persons are more likely to exhibit cognitive entrenchment. They are not necessarily fools. However, they become too committed to established and strongly held ideas to develop new ones. Or, as psychologists Alison Gropnik and Tom Griffiths put it, "Why does creativity generally tend to decline as we age? One reason may be that as we grow older, we know more. That's mostly an advantage, of course. But it also may lead us to ignore evidence that contradicts what we already think. We become too set in our ways to change."[16]

Weinberg and Galenson offer experimental evidence supporting this perspective. They find that in the field of economics, experimental innovators peaked at an average age of fifty-seven while conceptual innovators peaked at an average age of twenty-nine.[17] The most famous conceptual innovator in modern science, Albert Einstein, was thirty-six in the year 1905 when he published the four papers that laid the foundations of modern physics. As he grew older, though, Einstein himself showed signs of cognitive entrenchment and was inclined to reject new perspectives in such areas as quantum theory that, ironically, had been inspired by his own work.

Of course, if future technologies succeed in greatly increasing the human life-span, the same or related technologies might also overcome the current limits on intellectual creativity and productivity. For the present, we can only observe that as humans age their intellectual capacities, especially their ability to see the world in new ways, wane markedly. If this idea holds true, the world of immortals would include even fewer Einsteins than the current world. One is reminded of the Greek idea of Hades, a gray world in which souls exist for all eternity but without purpose, hope, or change.

New Forms of Society

A third question is whether a world without death would allow the possibility of social or political change. Perhaps a society of immortals would be perfect, but just in case it possessed faults, would change be possible? Again, such a society has never existed, so we cannot be certain of the answer. It is, however, worth taking note of one fact. Generally speaking social and political change is driven by the young. As people age, they seem more likely to accept established ways of doing things and less likely to consider alternatives. Take the case of the American Revolution and the construction of a new system of government. America's founders were very young. In 1776, Thomas Jefferson, author of the Declaration of Independence, was thirty-three; James Madison, future president and principle author of the Constitution, was twenty-five; Alexander Hamilton, constitutional theorist and future founder of the Federalist Party, was twenty-one; important revolutionary leaders such as John Marshall, future chief justice of the U.S. Supreme Court, was twenty-one; James

Monroe, Charles Pinckney, and the Marquis de Lafayette were all eighteen.

Youth is the author of political change. In the present world, old (albeit sometimes wise) people die and make room for young people with new (even if sometimes foolish) ways of looking at things. Would immortals make room for youth? Change is not necessarily progress but is a necessary condition for progress. Would there be a place for change in a world of immortals?

Olympus

Finally, as a thought experiment, let us consider the virtuousness of a world of immortals, a world in which death has been banished. Perhaps such a world would be idyllic, just, and peaceful, similar to religious visions of heaven. But, unfortunately, there are other possibilities as well. In a world of immortals or near-immortals political struggle and strife might become even more vicious than in the present world. For one vision of life in the absence of death, consider Olympus and its immortals. Immortality allowed the Olympians an eternity in which to comport themselves in a vindictive, impulsive, and spiteful manner. Having little to fear, the Olympians were frequently cruel to vulnerable mortals. Indeed, the Olympians resembled a tenured university faculty. The major gods could wound but not kill one another and sought amusement, and relief from boredom, by inflicting casual cruelties upon lesser beings. A world without death might not be a utopia. Perhaps only in death is there hope.

Notes

CHAPTER ONE. THE THANATOTIC CONTRACT

1. Sheldon Solomon, Jeff Greenberg, and Tom Pyszczynski, *The Worm at the Core: On the Role of Death in Life* (New York: Penguin, 2015). Also Clay Routledge and Matthew Vess, eds., *Handbook of Terror Management Theory* (Cambridge, MA: Academic Press, 2019).
2. Baudrillard makes a similar point. See Jean Baudrillard, *Symbolic Exchange and Death*, trans. Iain Hamilton Grant (London: Sage, 1993), 165.
3. Achille Mbembe, *Necropolitics* (Durham, NC: Duke University Press, 2019).
4. Michel Foucault, *The History of Sexuality*, vol. 1 (New York: Vintage, 1990), 138.
5. Effie Bendann, *Death Customs: An Analytical Study of Burial Rights* (New York: Knopf, 1930).
6. Alan F. Segal, *Life after Death* (New York: Doubleday, 2003), ch. 1.
7. Geoffrey Conrad and Arthur Demarest, *The Dynamics of Aztec and Inca Expansionism* (New York: Cambridge University Press, 1984).

8. Martin Heidegger, *Being and Time*, trans. John Macquarrie and Edward Robinson (New York: Harper and Row, 1962), 298.

9. Norbert Elias, *The Loneliness of Dying*, trans. Edmund Jephcott (New York: Continuum, 2001), 12.

10. Ernest Becker, *Escape from Evil* (New York: Free Press, 1975), ch. 5.

11. Robert J. Lifton, *Revolutionary Immortality: Mao Tse-tung and the Chinese Cultural Revolution* (New York: Random House, 1968), 32.

12. Lifton, *Revolutionary Immortality*.

13. Robert Kaplan, "The Lure of Nationalism," RealClearWorld, March 6, 2014, https://www.realclearworld.com/articles/2014/03/06/the_lure_of_nationalism.html.

14. Milovan R. Subotić and Miroslav Mitrović, "Hybrid Nature of Extremism: Cohesive Characteristics of Ethno-Nationalism and Religious Extremism as Generators of Balkan Insecurity," *Vojno Delo* 70.1 (2018): 22–33, http://www.isi.mod.gov.rs/multimedia/dodaci/vojno_delo_2018_1_subotic_1534759646.pdf.

15. Sheldon Solomon and Sharlynn Thompson, "Secular Cultural Worldviews," in Routledge and Vess, *Handbook of Terror Management Theory*, 289.

16. Helmut Walser Smith, "Nation and Nationalism," in *Germany, 1800-1870*, ed. Jonathan Sperber (New York: Oxford University Press, 2004), 231.

17. Leo Alexander, "Sociopsychologic Structure of the SS," *Archives of Neurology and Psychiatry* 59.626 (1948): 628–634.

18. Noor Dahri, "Suicide Terrorism, Root Causes and Effects," *Jewish News*, October 9, 2016, https://blogs.timesofisrael.com/suicide-terrorism-root-causes-effects/.

19. Maurice Halbwachs, *The Causes of Suicide*, trans. Harold Goldblatt (New York: Free Press, 1978), 293.

20. Baudrillard, *Symbolic Exchange and Death*, 149.

21. G. Stanley Hall, "Thanatophobia and Immortality," *American Journal of Psychology* 26.4 (October 1915): 560.

22. Becker, *Escape from Evil*, ch. 8.

23. Chad O'Carroll, "Is North Korea Now Erasing History?," *Telegraph*, December 16, 2013, http://www.telegraph.co.uk/news/worldnews/asia/northkorea/10520935/Is-North-Korea-now-erasing-history.html.

24. Becker, *Escape from Evil*, 102.

25. Geoffrey W. Conrad and Arthur A. Demarest, "The Aztec Imperial Expansion," in *Religion and Empire: The Dynamics of Aztec and Inca Expansionism* (Cambridge: Cambridge University Press, 1984), 41.

26. Scott K. Radford and Peter H. Bloch, "Ritual, Mythology and Consumption after a Celebrity Death," in *Death in a Consumer Culture*, ed. Susan Dobscha (London: Routledge, 2016), 108–122.

27. Fritz Stern, *Gold and Iron: Bismarck, Bleichroder and the Building of the German Empire* (New York: Vintage, 1977); Daniel Goldhagen, *Hitler's Willing Executioners: Ordinary Germans and the Holocaust* (New York: Vintage, 1997), 166.

28. Becker, *Escape from Evil*, ch. 10.

29. "The Antichrist and Donald Trump?" Donald Trump Is Evil, https://istrumpevil.com/faq/trump-and-the-antichrist/. The "About Us" section of the site asserts, "It is not only our goal, but our duty to stop him."

30. Benjamin Ginsberg, *Presidential Government* (New Haven, CT: Yale University Press, 2016), 392.

31. Solomon and Thompson, "Secular Cultural Worldviews," 290.

32. Leo Braudy, *The Frenzy of Renown: Fame and Its History* (New York: Vintage, 1997), ch. 2.

33. Braudy, *Frenzy of Renown*, 378.

34. Douglas Adair, *Fame and the Founding Fathers* (New York: W. W. Norton, 1974), ch. 1. Also Peter R. Henriques, "The Final Struggle between George Washington and the Grim King: Washington's Attitude toward Death and Afterlife," *Virginia Magazine of History and Biography* 107.1 (Winter 1999): 73–97.

35. Sir Francis Bacon, *Essays* (New York: Cosimo Classics, 2007).

36. Friedrich Nietzsche, *Thus Spake Zarathustra* (New York: Oxford University Press, 2009), part 1, xl.

37. Michael Sledge, *Soldier Dead: How We Recover, Identify, Bury & Honor Our Military Fallen* (New York: Columbia University Press, 2005).

38. Don Herzog, Defaming the Dead (New Haven, CT: Yale University Press, 2017), 168.

39. Becker, *Escape from Evil*, ch. 8.

CHAPTER TWO. THE SECULARIZATION OF DEATH

1. Carl Schmitt, *Political Theology*, trans. George Schwabb (Chicago: University of Chicago Press, 2005), ch. 3.
2. Zygmunt Bauman, *Mortality, Immortality & Other Life Strategies* (Stanford: Stanford University Press, 1992), ch. 4.
3. Sam Parnia, *Erasing Death* (New York: HarperOne, 2014).
4. Thomas W. Laqueur, *The Work of the Dead: A Cultural History of Mortal Remains* (Princeton, NJ: Princeton University Press, 2015), 116.
5. Ivan Illich, *Medical Nemesis: The Expropriation of Health* (New York: Pantheon, 1982), 176.
6. Quoted in Laqueur, *Work of the Dead*, 156.
7. Laqueur, *Work of the Dead*, 195.
8. Philippe Ariès, *The Hour of Our Death* (New York: Random House, 1971), 479.
9. Bruce S. Elliott, "Proclaiming Modernity in the Monument Trade," in *Death in a Consumer Culture*, ed. Susan Dobscha (London: Routledge, 2016), 13–42. See also Jessica Mitford, *The American Way of Death* (New York: Vintage Books, 2000).
10. Laqueur, *Work of the Dead*, 7.
11. Effie Bendann, *Death Customs: An Analytical Study of Burial Rites* (New York: Knopf, 1930), 121.
12. E. A. Wallis Budge, ed., *The Egyptian Book of the Dead* (New York: Dover, 1967).
13. "Coroner," Britannica, https://www.britannica.com/topic/coroner.
14. I. R. Hill, "The Coroner—12th and 13th Century Development of the Office," *Medical Science Law* 30.2 (1990): 133–197.
15. Bridget Heos, *Blood, Bullets and Bones* (New York: HarperCollins, 2016), 32.
16. Katherine Ramsland, *Beating the Devil's Game: A History of Forensic Science and Criminal Investigation* (New York: Penguin, 2007), 9.
17. Gregory G. Davis, "Mind Your Manners, Part 1: History of Death Certification and Manner of Death Classification," *American Journal of Forensic Medicine and Pathology* 18.3 (September 1997): 219–223.
18. "Statutes of the Realm, 1101 to 1713," The Statutes Project, vol. 1, Henry III to Edward III.

19. Alan Macfarlane, "Illegitimacy and Illegitimates in English History," in *Bastardy and Its Comparative History*, ed. Peter Laslett, Karla Oosterveen, and Richard M. Smith (London: Arnold, 1980), 71–85.

20. Associated Press, "California Women Gave Birth to Each Other's Babies after IVF Mix-up," *Guardian*, November 9, 2021, https://www.theguardian.com/us-news/2021/nov/09/california-women-gave-birth-to-each-others-babies-after-ivf-mix-up.

21. 49 Cal. Rptr. 2d 694 (Ct. App. 1996).

22. In re Marriage of Buzzanca, 72 Cal. Rptr. 2d 280, 287 (Ct. App. 1998).

23. Eric Ehrenreich, *The Nazi Ancestral Proof: Genealogy, Racial Science and the Final Solution* (Bloomington: Indiana University Press, 2007).

24. Bryan Mark Rigg, *Hitler's Jewish Soldiers: The Untold Story of Nazi Racial Laws and Men of Jewish Descent in the German Military* (Lawrence: University Press of Kansas, 2002).

25. Guenter B. Risse, *Mending Bodies, Saving Souls: A History of Hospitals* (New York: Oxford University Press, 1999), 218.

26. Risse, *Mending Bodies*, 150.

27. Ariès, *Hour of Our Death*, 570.

28. Paul Slack, *Plague* (New York: Oxford University Press, 2012), 75, 76.

29. Dorothy Porter, *Health, Civilization and the State* (London: Routledge, 1999), 39.

30. Michael B. A. Oldstone, *Viruses, Plagues and History* (New York: Oxford University Press, 2010), ch. 4.

31. Clay S. Jenkinson, "How Jefferson and Franklin Helped End Smallpox in America," *Governing*, April 29, 2020, https://www.governing.com/context/How-Jefferson-and-Franklin-Helped-End-Smallpox-in-America.html.

32. Oldstone, *Viruses, Plagues and History*, 78, 79.

33. Jenkinson, "How Jefferson and Franklin Helped."

34. Oldstone, *Viruses, Plagues and History*, 77.

35. Bauman, *Mortality, Immortality*, 137.

36. Bauman, *Mortality, Immortality*, 138.

37. Michael Lewis, *The Premonition: A Pandemic Story* (New York: W. W. Norton, 2021).

38. Don B. Kates, "Guns and Public Health: Epidemic of Violence or

Pandemic of Propaganda?,'" in *Armed*, ed. Gary Kleck and Don B. Kates (New York: Prometheus Books, 2001), 31–85.

39. Neil Marr and Tim Field, *Bullycide: Death at Playtime; An Exposé of Child Suicide Caused by Bullying* (New York: Gardners Books, 2000).

40. Michael Fitzpatrick, *The Tyranny of Health* (New York: Routledge, 2001).

41. Chris Buckley, Vivian Wang, and Keith Bradsher, "China's Strict Covid Controls May Outlast Covid: Adapting Health App to Tighten Xi's Grip," *New York Times*, January 30, 2022, 1.

42. Jacob Sullum, "The Tyranny of Public Health," *Medical Sentinel* 4.4 (May/June 1999): 100–102.

43. "Constitution," World Health Organization. https://www.who.int/about/accountability/governance/constitution.

44. Jean Baudrillard, *Symbolic Exchange and Death*, trans. Iain Hamilton Grant (London: Sage, 1993), 174.

45. Robin M. Henig, *The People's Health* (Washington, DC: Joseph Henry Press, 1996).

CHAPTER THREE. THE RIGHTS OF THE DEAD

1. Michael Shermer, *Heavens on Earth* (New York: St. Martin's Press, 2018), chs. 5 and 6.

2. Ron Charles, "Boy Who Came Back from Heaven Actually Didn't; Books Recalled," *Washington Post*, January 15, 2015, https://www.washingtonpost.com/news/arts-and-entertainment/wp/2015/01/15/boy-who-came-back-from-heaven-going-back-to-publisher.

3. See Kirsten Rabe Smolensky, "Rights of the Dead," *Hofstra Law Review* 37.3 (Spring 2009): 763–803.

4. Thomas Scanlon, "Rights and Interests," in *Arguments for a Better World: Essays in Honor of Amartya Sen*, vol. 1, ed. Kaushik Basu and Ravi Kanbur (New York: Oxford University Press, 2008), 68–79.

5. Daniel Sperling, *Posthumous Interests: Legal and Ethical Perspectives* (New York: Cambridge University Press, 2008).

6. Aristotle, *Nicomachean Ethics*, ed. Roger Crisp (New York: Cambridge University Press, 2000), 16.

7. Quoted in Sperling, *Posthumous Interests*, 1.

8. Ivan Illich, *Medical Nemesis: The Expropriation of Health* (New York: Pantheon, 1982), 187.

9. Fred O. Smith, "The Constitution after Death," *Columbia Law Review* 120.6 (October 2020): 1471–1548.

10. Ernest Becker, *Escape from Evil* (New York: Free Press, 1975), 3.

11. Robert Sitkoff and Jesse Dukeminier, *Wills, Trusts and Estates*, 10th ed. (New York: Walters Kluwer, 2017), 3.

12. *Restatement (Third) of Property, Wills and Other Donative Transfers* (Philadelphia: American Law Institute, 2003), §10.1.

13. 315 N.E. 2d 825 (1974).

14. 388 U.S. 1 (1967).

15. 334 U.S. 1 (1948).

16. Ray D. Madoff, *Immortality and the Law: The Rising Power of the American Dead* (New Haven, CT: Yale University Press, 2010), 75.

17. J. Peder Zane, "The Rise of Incentive Trusts; Six Feet Under and Overbearing," *New York Times*, March 12, 1995, https://www.nytimes.com/1995/03/12/weekinreview/ideas-trends-the-rise-of-incentive-trusts-six-feet-under-and-overbearing.html.

18. Madoff, *Immortality and the Law*, 78.

19. Madoff, *Immortality and the Law*, 85.

20. Lawrence M. Friedman, *Dead Hands: A Social History of Wills, Trusts and Inheritance Law* (Stanford: Stanford University Press, 2009), 71.

21. Madoff, *Immortality and the Law*, 90.

22. Sitkoff and Dukeminier, *Wills, Trusts and Estates*, 767.

23. Sitkoff and Dukeminier, *Wills, Trusts and Estates*, 773.

24. Philip Shenon, "Settlement Reached on Bequest to P.L.O.," *New York Times*, February 7, 1984, https://www.nytimes.com/1984/02/07/nyregion/settlement-reached-on-bequest-to-plo.html.

25. 382 U.S. 296 (1966).

26. 396 U.S. 435 (1970).

27. Smith, "Constitution after Death," 1488.

28. 483 F. Supp. 62 (D. Haw. 1979).

29. 481 U.S. 704 (1987).

30. Friedman, *Dead Hands*, ch. 4.

31. Smolensky, "Rights of the Dead," 783.

32. 20 Cal. Rptr. 2d 282 (1996).

33. 760 N.E. 2d 257 (Mass. 2002).

34. 541 U.S. 157 (2004).

35. Schuyler v. Curtis, 42 N.E. 22 (N.Y. 1895).

36. Clay Calvert, "The Privacy of Death: An Emergent Jurisprudence and Legal Rebuke to Media Exploitation and a Voyeuristic Culture," *Loyola of Los Angeles Entertainment Law Review* 26.2 (2006): 136, 139.

37. New York Times Co. v. City of New York Fire Department, 829 N.E. 2d 266 (N.Y. 2005).

38. Reid v. Pierce County, 961 P.2d 333 (Wash. 1998).

39. Calvert, "Privacy of Death," 158.

40. Madoff, *Immortality and the Law*, 128.

41. Madoff, *Immortality and the Law*, 129.

42. "Health Information of Deceased Individuals," U.S. Department of Health and Human Services, https://www.hhs.gov/hipaa/for-professionals/privacy/guidance/health-information-of-deceased-individuals/index.html.

43. Don Herzog, *Defaming the Dead* (New Haven, CT: Yale University Press, 2017), 250.

44. Katherine Q. Seelye, "Mudd's Family Renews Effort to Clear His Name," SFGate.com, September 4, 2002, https://www.sfgate.com/news/article/Mudd-s-family-renews-effort-to-clear-his-name-2774564.php.

45. Smith, "Constitution after Death," 1512.

46. Smith, "Constitution after Death," 1513.

47. Bo Zao, "Posthumous Reputation and Posthumous Privacy in China: The Dead, the Law, and Social Transition," *Brooklyn Journal of International Law* 39.1 (2014): 270–352.

48. Robert Strand, "Guide to Deceased Celebrity Licensing," *Branding Insider Strategy*, July 5, 2010, https://www.brandingstrategyinsider.com/10748/#.YHdVmSWSmUk.

49. Sitkoff and Dukeminier, *Wills, Trusts and Estates*, 34.

50. Madoff, *Immortality and the Law*, 136.

51. Madoff, *Immortality and the Law*, 142.

52. Madoff, *Immortality and the Law*, 150.

53. Jani McCutcheon, "The Honor of the Dead—the Moral Right of

Integrity Post-Mortem," *Federal Law Review* 42.3 (September 2013): 494.

54. Quoted in McCutcheon, "Honor of the Dead," 498.

55. McCutcheon, "Honor of the Dead," 500.

56. Fahmy v. Jay-Z, USDC, C.D. (Calif., October 21, 2015).

57. McCutcheon, "Honor of the Dead," 486.

58. Herzog, *Defaming the Dead*, ch. 5.

59. 1 Me. 226 (1821).

60. Smith, "Constitution after Death," 1493.

61. "Johnny Depp Spent $3m Blasting Hunter S. Thompson's Ashes from Cannon, Ex-Managers Claim," *Guardian*, February 1, 2017, https://www.theguardian.com/film/2017/feb/01/johnny-depp-spent-3m-blasting-hunter-s-thompson-ashes-from-cannon-ex-managers-claim.

62. Madoff, *Immortality and the Law*, 15.

63. Smith, "Constitution after Death," 1497.

64. Moore v. Regents of the University of California, 793 P.2d 479 (Calif. 1980).

65. Amy Goldstein, "White House Set to Change Rules on Fetal Tissue Research," *Washington Post*, April 16, 2021, A9.

66. Alberto B. Lopez and Frederick E. Vars, "Wrongful Living," *Iowa Law Review* 104 (2019): 1921.

67. "Practice Parameters: Assessment and Management of Patients in the Persistent Vegetative State: Summary Statement," *Neurology* 45.5 (1995): 1015–1018, doi:10.1212/wnl.45.5.1015, PMID 7746375.

68. Schloendorff v. Society of New York Hospital, 105 N.E. 92 (N.Y. 1914).

69. Lopez and Vars, "Wrongful Living," 1931.

70. 497 U.S. 261 (1990).

71. Rebecca Dresser, "Treatment Decisions and Changing Selves," *Journal of Medical Ethics*, 41.12 (2014): 975–976, https://jme.bmj.com/content/41/12/975.

72. North Carolina is an example. Lynn Bonner and Yanqi Xu, "When a Hospital Is Overwhelmed with COVID-19 Patients, Deciding Who Gets Critical Care," *NC Policy Watch*, February 2, 2021, http://www.ncpolicywatch.com/2021/02/02/

when-a-hospital-is-overwhelmed-with-covid-19-patients-deciding-who-gets-critical-care.

73. Ernest Becker, *The Denial of Death* (New York: Free Press, 1973). See also Sheldon Solomon, Jeff Greenberg, and Tom Pyszczynski, *The Worm at the Core: On the Role of Death in Life* (New York: Penguin, 2015).

74. Lucretius, *On the Nature of Things*, trans. Martin Ferguson Smith (New York: Hackett, 2001).

75. Effie Bendann, *Death Customs: An Analytical Study of Burial Rites* (New York: Knopf, 1930).

76. Zygmunt Bauman, *Mortality, Immortality & Other Life Strategies* (Stanford: Stanford University Press, 1992), ch. 4.

CHAPTER FOUR. THE POWER OF THE DEAD

1. Eccles. 9:5–6 (*The Complete Jewish Bible*, ch. 9, https://www.chabad.org/library/bible_cdo/aid/16470/jewish/Chapter-9.htm).

2. Thornton Wilder, *Our Town: A Play in Three Acts* (New York: HarperCollins Publishers, 2003), act 3, 1938.

3. For a discussion of the awareness of voters, see Christopher Achen and Larry Bartels, *Democracy for Realists* (Princeton, NJ: Princeton University Press, 2016).

4. Jennifer Bachner and Benjamin Ginsberg, *America's State Governments* (New York: Routledge, 2021), ch. 7.

5. Emile Durkheim, *Suicide* (New York: Routledge, 1970).

6. Maurice Halbwachs, *The Causes of Suicide*, trans. Harold Goldblatt (New York: Free Press, 1978), 292.

7. Kristen Renwick Monroe, *The Heart of Altruism* (Princeton, NJ: Princeton University Press, 1998).

8. Michael Berenbaum and Reuven Firestone, "The Theology of Martyrdom," in *Martyrdom: The Psychology, Theology and Politics of Self-Sacrifice*, ed. Rona M. Fields (Westport, CT: Praeger, 2004), 125.

9. Rona Fields, *Martyrdom* (New York: Praeger, 2004), 5.

10. Gail P. Streete, "Performing Christian Martyrdoms" in *Martyrdom, Self-Sacrifice and Self-Immolation: Religious Perspectives on Suicide*, ed. Margo Kitts (New York: Oxford University Press, 2018), 41.

11. Gregory Elder, "Professing Faith: Last Words of the Dying Range from Religious to Profound to Profane," *Redlands Daily Facts*, January 21, 2018, https://www.redlandsdailyfacts.com/2018/01/31/professing-faith-last-words-of-the-dying-range-from-religious-to-profound-to-profane/.

12. Elesnor Doumato, "Protestantism and Protestant Missions," in *Encyclopedia of the Middle East and North Africa*, ed. Philip Mattar (New York: Macmillan, 2004).

13. Berenbaum and Firestone, "Theology of Martyrdom," 141.

14. Mohammed M. Hafez, "Apologia for Suicide: Martyrdom in Contemporary Jihadist Discourse," in Kitts, *Martyrdom, Self-Sacrifice and Self-Immolation*, 131.

15. Robert A. Pape, *Dying to Win: The Strategic Logic of Suicide Terrorism* (New York: Random House, 2005), 61.

16. Pape, *Dying to Win*, 221.

17. Horace, *Odes*, 3.2.13.

18. "Nathan Hale," Wikiquote, https://en.wikiquote.org/wiki/Nathan_Hale.

19. The precise character of the events at the Alamo is open to question. See Bryan Burrough, Chris Tomlinson, and Jason Stanford, *Forget the Alamo: The Rise and Fall of an American Myth* (New York: Penguin, 2021).

20. Philip M. Taylor, *Munitions of the Mind: A History of Propaganda from the Ancient World to the Present Day*, 3rd ed. (Manchester: Manchester University Press, 2003), 31.

21. Taylor, *Munitions of the Mind*, 115.

22. Thomas Paine, *The Crisis*, December 23, 1776, USHistory.org, http://www.ushistory.org/paine/crisis/c-01.htm.

23. Carl von Clausewitz, *On War*, ed. Michael Howard and Peter Paret (Princeton: Princeton University Press, 1976), 591.

24. Charles Tilly, "War Making and State Making as Organized Crime," in *Bringing the State Back In*, ed. Peter Evans, Dietrich Rueschmeyer, and Theda Skocpol (Cambridge, MA: Harvard University Press, 1985), 169–186.

25. Ava Gail Cass, Elizabeth Frankenberg, Wayan Suriastini, and Duncan Thomas, "The Impact of Parental Death on Child Well-Being," *Demography* 51 (2014): 437–457.

26. Benjamin Ginsberg, *The Worth of War* (New York: Prometheus Books, 2014), 50.

27. Barrington Moore Jr., *The Social Origins of Dictatorship and Democracy* (Boston: Beacon Press, 1966).

28. Benjamin F. Jones and Benjamin A. Olken, "Hit or Miss? The Effect of Assassinations on Institutions and War," *American Economic Journal: Macroeconomics* 1.2 (July 2009): 55–87.

29. William H. McNeill, *Plagues and People* (New York: Anchor Books, 1977), ch. 5.

30. Paul Slack, *Plague* (New York: Oxford University Press, 2012), ch. 3.

31. Letter from James Madison to Thomas Jefferson, February 4, 1790, National Archives, https://founders.archives.gov.

32. James Q. Wilson, *Bureaucracy: What Government Agencies Do and Why They Do It* (New York: Basic Books, 1989), 91.

33. See Anita Huslin, "Grizzly Proposition Aims to Return Bears to Idaho," *Washington Post*, July 3, 2000, A3.

34. Harold Seidman, *Politics, Position and Power*, 5th ed. (New York: Oxford University Press, 1998), 138.

35. Seidman, *Politics, Position and Power*, 118.

36. Thomas Stanton, *Government Sponsored Enterprises: Mercantilist Corporations in the Modern World* (Washington, DC: American Enterprise Institute, 2000).

37. Friedrich Nietzsche, *Thus Spake Zarathustra* (New York: Oxford University Press, 2009).

38. Hannah Arendt, *Eichmann in Jerusalem* (New York: Penguin Classics, 2006).

39. Stanley Milgram, *Obedience to Authority*, (New York: Harper, 1974), 48.

40. Zygmunt Bauman, *Modernity and the Holocaust* (Ithaca, NY: Cornell University Press, 2000), 215.

41. An adiapharon was something declared indifferent, neither good nor evil, by the church. Bauman, *Modernity*, 215.

42. In recent years, the public's fear of crime, fueled by claims of ambitious politicians that their opponents were "soft on crime," did indeed play a role in the enactment of harsh sentencing policies and a decay of prison conditions. See David Garland, *The Culture of Control: Crime and Social Order in Contemporary Society* (Chicago: University of

Chicago Press, 2001). Also Jonathon Simon, *Governing through Crime: How the War on Crime Transformed American Democracy and Created a Culture of Fear* (New York: Oxford University Press, 2007).

43. William Dunning, *Reconstruction: Political and Economic, 1865–1877* (New York: Harper, 1907).

44. Geoffrey W. Conrad and Arthur A. Demarest, *Religion and Empire: The Dynamics of Aztec and Inca Expansionism* (Cambridge: Cambridge University Press, 1984), 186.

CHAPTER FIVE. OBLIVION

1. Edward M. Kennedy, "Address at the Public Memorial Service for Robert F. Kennedy" (eulogy, St. Patrick's Cathedral, NY, June 8, 1968).

2. Janice Hume, "Write Ill of the Dead?," *Conversation*, April 12, 2021, https://theconversation.com/write-ill-of-the-dead-obits-rarely-cross-that-taboo-as-they-look-for-the-positive-in-peoples-lives-158753.

3. Terrance G. Gabel, "Cheating Death via Social Self Immortalization," in *Death in a Consumer Culture*, ed. Susan Dobscha (London: Routledge, 2016), 138–169.

4. "Talk to the Newsroom: Obituaries Editor Bill McDonald," *New York Times*, September 25, 2006, https://www.nytimes.com/2006/09/25/business/media/25asktheeditors.html.

5. Thomas W. Laqueur, *The Work of the Dead: A Cultural History of Mortal Remains* (Princeton, NJ: Princeton University Press, 2015), ch. 5.

6. Harold Mylum, *Mortuary Monuments and Burial Grounds of the Historic Period* (New York: Kluwer, 2004). See also Hakan Cengiz and Dennis W. Rook, "Voluntary Simplicity in the Final Rite of Passage: Death," in Dobscha, *Death in a Consumer Culture*, 123–134.

7. Mary Jordan and Kevin Sullivan, "Alone in Death," *Washington Post*, September 17, 2021, https://www.washingtonpost.com/nation/2021/09/17/alone-death.

8. Kenna Quinet, Samuel Nunn, and Alfarena Ballew, "Who Are the Unclaimed Dead?," *Journal of Forensic Sciences* 61.2 (January 2016): 131–139.

9. Dean Olsen, "Homeless Man in Sangamon County Dumpster Accidentally Crushed to Death inside Garbage Truck," *State Journal-Register*, December 9, 2021, https://www.sj-r.com/story/news/2021/12/09/workers-sangamon-county-waste-management-station-discover-dead-body/6451993001.

10. Quoted in Jordan and Sullivan, "Alone in Death."

11. Michael T. Keene, *New York's Hart Island: A Cemetery of Strangers* (New York: History Press, 2019).

12. Bill Twomey, *The Bronx in Bits and Pieces* (New York: Rooftop Publishing, 2017).

13. Brody Ford, "The Biggest Public Graveyard in the U.S. Is Becoming a Park," *Bloomberg City Lab*, October 15, 2021, https://www.bloomberg.com/news/features/2021-10-15/nyc-s-biggest-public-graveyard-hart-island-gets-remodel.

14. Adam F. C. Fletcher, "A History of the Potter's Field in North Omaha," North Omaha History, September 4, 2019, https://northomahahistory.com/2019/09/04/a-history-of-the-potters-field-in-north-omaha.

15. Michael Waters, No One Really Knows What to Do with All of America's Unclaimed Corpses," *Atlantic*, February 12, 2019, https://www.theatlantic.com/health/archive/2019/02/unclaimed-bodies-problem/582625.

16. Simon Davis, "This Is What Happens to Unclaimed Bodies in Washington, DC," VICE Digital, April 6, 2015, https://www.vice.com/en/article/9bze43/this-is-what-happens-to-unclaimed-bodies-in-washington-dc-406.

17. Christopher Payne, *Asylum: Inside the Closed World of State Mental Hospitals* (Cambridge, MA: MIT Press, 2009).

18. Mark L. Ruffalo, "The American Mental Asylum: A Remnant of History," *Psychology Today*, July 13, 2018, https://www.psychologytoday.com/us/blog/freud-fluoxetine/201807/the-american-mental-asylum-remnant-history.

19. Erving Goffman, *Asylums* (New York: Random House, 1961).

20. John Kuroski, "Thousands of Bodies Found Buried under 19th Century Mississippi Insane Asylum," All That's Interesting, May 8, 2017, https://allthatsinteresting.com/mississippi-state-asylum.

21. Stewart Ain, "Numbers Mark the Graves at a Former Psychiatric Hospital's Jewish Cemetery," *Washington Jewish Week*, December 16, 2021, 10.
22. Allison Meier, "America's Abandoned Insane Asylum Cemeteries," *Atlas Obscura*, October 27, 2014, https://www.atlasobscura.com.
23. M. Benezich, "Fortune and Misfortune of the Cemetery of the Lunatics of Cadillac," *Histoire des Sciences Medicales* 42.1 (January 1, 2008): 71–80.
24. Erin Millions and Ian Mosby, "Canada's Residential Schools Were a Horror, " *Scientific American*, August 1, 2021, https://www.scientificamerican.com/article/canadas-residential-schools-were-a-horror.
25. Mariah Balington, "Burial Sites at 53 Indian Schools So Far," *Washington Post*, May 13, 2022, A2.
26. E. Ann Carson, *Mortality in State and Federal Prisons, 2001–2019—Statistical Tables* (Washington, DC: Bureau of Justice Statistics, December 2021), https://bjs.ojp.gov/library/publications/mortality-state-and-federal-prisons-2001-2019-statistical-tables.
27. Connor Sheets, "Death behind Bars: Buried in Alabama's Prison Cemeteries, Life Sentences Last beyond Death," AL.com, August 6, 2017, https://www.al.com.
28. "Arkansas Prison Said Graveyard of Murdered Men," *Desert Sun*, January 30, 1968, https://cdnc.ucr.edu.
29. "Captain Joe Byrd Cemetery," Find a Grave, https://www.findagrave.com/cemetery/641459/captain-joe-byrd-cemetery.
30. Craig Pittman, 'Graveyard Is Filling with the Forgotten," *Tampa Bay Times*, October 7, 2005, https://www.tampabay.com/archive/1994/05/22/graveyard-is-filling-with-the-forgotten.
31. Tom Dart, "'Building over History': The Prison Graveyard Buried under a Texas Suburb," *Guardian*, June 22, 2019, https://www.theguardian.com/us-news/2019/jun/22/sugar-land-texas-95-burial-ground.
32. Achille Mbembe, *Necropolitics* (Durham, NC: Duke University Press, 2019).
33. Ernst Bornstein, *The Long Night* (New Milford, CT: Toby Press, 2016). The German term means "Muslim" and is derived from the image of

an individual prostrate on the ground in prayer.

34. Ethan Gutman, *The Slaughter: Mass Killings, Organ Harvesting, and China's Secret Solution to Its Dissident Problem* (New York: Prometheus, 2014).

35. Michael Sledge, *Soldier Dead: How We Recover, Identify, Bury & Honor Our Military Fallen* (New York: Columbia University Press, 2005), 34.

36. Sledge, *Soldier Dead*, 45.

37. Jalaa Marey, "Israel Releases Syrian Prisoners as 'Gesture' for Return of Body of IDF Soldier 37 Years Later," *i24 News*, April 28, 2019, https://www.i24news.tv.

38. Joe Davidson, "Bittersweet Vindication for an Army Widow," *Washington Post*, April 23, 2022, A2.

39. Sledge, *Soldier Dead*, 241.

40. Megan Palin, "'Crack, Crack and My Back Broke': Former Prisoners Reveal Horrific Torture Taking Place in Chinese Prisons," *Sun of Australia*, September 16, 2016, https://www.thesun.co.uk/news/1799086/former-prisoners-reveal-horrific-torture-taking-place-in-chinese-prisons.

41. Laqueur, *Work of the Dead*.

42. Leighann C. Neilson and Delphin A. Muise, "Great Granny Lives On: Pursuing Immortality through Family History Research," in Dobscha, *Death in a Consumer Culture*, 170–183.

CHAPTER SIX. RESURRECTION

1. Ronald Bishop, "In the Grand Scheme of Things: An Exploration of the Meaning of Genealogical Research," *Journal of Popular Culture* 41.3 (2008): 393–412, https://onlinelibrary.wiley.com/doi/full/10.1111/j.1540-5931.2008.00527.x.

2. 1 Sam. 28:15–20 (The Complete Hebrew Bible, https://www.chabad.org/library/bible_cdo/aid/63255/jewish/The-Bible-with-Rashi.htm).

3. Quoted in Georg Luck, *Arcana Mundi: Magic and the Occult in the Greek and Roman Worlds* (Baltimore: Johns Hopkins University Press, 2006), 251.

4. Luck, *Arcana Mundi*, 256.

5. Homer, *The Odyssey*, 11.556–558.

6. R. C. Symes, "Myths Surrounding the Birth of Jesus," Progressive Christianity, January 25, 2011, https://progressivechristianity.org/resource/myths-surrounding-the-birth-of-jesus.

7. Bart D. Ehrman, *How Jesus Became God* (New York: HarperCollins, 2014).

8. Dag Oisteen Endsjo, *Greek Resurrection Beliefs and the Success of Christianity* (New York: Palgrave Macmillan, 2009), ch. 7.

9. Aviva Orenstein, "Her Last Words: Dying Declarations and Modern Confrontation Jurisprudence," *University of Illinois Law Review* 5 (2010): 1411–1460, https://www.illinoislawreview.org/wp-content/ilr-content/articles/2010/5/Orenstein.pdf.

10. 168 Eng. Rep. 352 (1789).

11. 146 U.S. 140 (1892).

12. Carver v. United States, 164 U.S. 897 (1897).

13. Brendan J. Koerner, "Last Words: Why Are We So Sure That Death and Honesty Go Together?," *Legal Affairs*, November/December 2002, https://www.legalaffairs.org/issues/November-December-2002.

14. Song Ci, *The Washing Away of Wrongs* (Ann Arbor: University of Michigan Center for Chinese Studies, 1981).

15. Katherine Ramsland, *Beating the Devil's Game: A History of Forensic Science and Criminal Investigation* (New York: Penguin, 2007), 15.

16. Kathy Mirakovitz and Jay A. Siegler, *Forensic Science*, 4th ed. (Boca Raton, FL: CRC Press, 2022), 10.

17. Gary Cordner, "The Myth That Science Solves Crimes," in *Demystifying Crime and Criminal Justice*, ed. Robert M. Bohm and Jeffery T. Walker (New York: Oxford University Press, 2013), 157–163.

18. Daniel Ogden, *Greek and Roman Necromancy* (Princeton, NJ: Princeton University Press, 2001), ch. 15. For a discussion of medieval necromancy, see Richard Kieckhefer, *Forbidden Rites* (University Park: Pennsylvania State University Press, 1997).

19. Ogden, *Greek and Roman Necromancy*, 196–198.

20. Alison Flood, "Jane Austen Biographer Discovers 'Lost Portrait,'" *Guardian*, December 5, 2011, https://www.theguardian.com/books/2011/dec/05/jane-austen-lost-portrait.

21. Hannah Beech, "China's President Sets All Party Members Homework to Read Old Report by Chairman Mao," *Time*, February

29, 2016, https://time.com.

22. David Herbert Donald, *Lincoln Reconsidered* (New York: Vintage, 1947), ch. 1, p. 3.

23. Quoted in Thomas DiLorenzo, "How the Lincoln Myth Was Hatched," LewRockwell.com, July 22, 2010, https://www.lewrockwell.com/2010/07/thomas-dilorenzo/the-first-dictator-president.

24. Quoted in DiLorenzo, "How the Lincoln Myth."

25. Carl Sandburg, *Abraham Lincoln: The Prairie Years and the War Years* (New York: Harcourt, Brace and World, 1954), 446.

26. Shelby Foote, *The Civil War* (New York: Vintage Books, 1958), 832.

27. Gabor Boritt, *The Gettysburg Gospel: The Lincoln Speech That Nobody Knows* (New York: Simon and Schuster, 2005), ch. 7.

28. Boritt, *Gettysburg Gospel*, ch. 7.

29. Abraham Lincoln, "The Gettysburg Address," Abraham Lincoln Online, https://www.abrahamlincolnonline.org/lincoln/speeches/gettysburg.htm.

30. Ibram X. Kendi and Keisha N. Blain, *Four Hundred Souls: A Community History of African America, 1619–2019* (New York: One World, 2021).

31. The Rise and Fall of Jim Crow, "D. W. Griffith's *The Birth of a Nation* (1915)," PBS, http://www.pbs.org/wnet/jimcrow/stories_events_birth.html.

32. William Dunning, *Reconstruction: Political and Economic, 1865–1877* (New York: Harper, 1907).

33. Eric Foner, *Reconstruction: America's Unfinished Revolution* (New York: Harper, 1988), xxii.

34. Nikole Hannah-Jones, Caitlin Roper, Ilena Silverman, and Jake Silverstien, eds., *The 1619 Project: A New Origin Story* (New York: One World Books, 2021).

35. Peter Novick, *The Holocaust in American Life* (New York: Mariner Books, 2000).

36. Robert Shogan, *Prelude to Catastrophe: FDR's Jews and the Menace of Nazism* (Chicago: Ivan Dee, 2010).

37. Leon W. Wells, *Who Speaks for the Vanquished?* (Lausanne, Switzerland: Peter Lang Publisher, 1988), 154.

38. Rafael Medoff, *The Deafening Silence* (New York: Carol Publishing

Group, 1986), ch. 7.

39. See Wells, *Who Speaks*, ch. 9.

40. Benjamin Ginsberg, *How the Jews Defeated Hitler* (Lanham, MD: Rowman and Littlefield, 2013), ch. 2.

41. Bea Stadtler, *The Holocaust: A History of Courage and Resistance* (New York: Behrman House, 1974), 30.

42. Stadtler, *The Holocaust*.

43. Ginsberg, *How the Jews Defeated Hitler*.

44. Wells, *Who Speaks*, ch. 7.

45. Michael Shermer, *Heavens on Earth* (New York: St. Martin's, 2018), ch. 8.

46. For a review of the issues, see Christopher James Ryan, "Saving Those Who Don't Wish to Be Saved," *Monash Bioethics Review* 15.2 (April 2014): 44–46.

AFTERWORD. DEATH AND CHANGE

1. "Phaedo," in *The Trial and Examination of Socrates*, trans. Peter George (London: Folio Society, 1972), 103.

2. Ernest Becker, *The Denial of Death* (New York: Free Press, 1973), 11.

3. Michael Bultman and Jamie Arndt, "Physical Health under the Shadow of Mortality: The Terror Management Health Model," in *Handbook of Terror Management Theory*, ed. Clay Routledge and Matthew Vess (Cambridge, MA: Academic Press, 2019), 369–390.

4. Discussed in Sheldon Solomon, Jeff Greenberg, and Tom Pyszczynski, *The Worm at the Core: On the Role of Death in Life* (New York: Penguin, 2015), 221.

5. Becker, *Denial of Death*, 12.

6. Max More and Natasha Vita-More, eds., *The Transhumanist Reader: Classical and Contemporary Essays on the Science, Technology, and Philosophy of the Human Future* (New York: Wiley-Blackwell, 2013).

7. Philip Ball, "The God Quest: Why Humans Long for Immortality," *New Statesman*, July 30, 2015, https://www.newstatesman.com/long-reads/2015/07/god-quest-why-humans-long-immortality.

8. Bruce Bueno De Mesquita and Alistair Smith, *Dictator's Handbook: Why Bad Behavior Is Almost Always Good Politics* (New York: Public Affairs

Press, 2012).

9. Thomas Hobbes, *Leviathan* (New York: Collier, 1962), 80.

10. Richard Shenkman, *Presidential Ambition* (New York: Harper, 1999), xii.

11. Matthew A. Crenson and Benjamin Ginsberg, *Presidential Power: Unchecked and Unbalanced* (New York: W. W. Norton, 2007).

12. Economist Intelligence Unit, *Democracy Index 2020* (London: Economist Intelligence Unit, 2020), https://www.eiu.com/n/campaigns/democracy-index-2020/.

13. Benjamin F. Jones and Benjamin A. Olken, "Hit or Miss? The Effect of Assassinations on Institutions and War," *American Economic Journal: Macroeconomics* 1.2 (July 2009): 55–87.

14. Kenneth J. Gilhooly and Mary L. M. Gilhooly, *Aging and Creativity* (New York: Academic Press, 2021), ch. 3.

15. David W. Galenson, "The Nature of Creativity in Old Age" (working paper no. 2019-67, University of Chicago, Becker-Friedman Institute, May 2019), https://bfi.uchicago.edu/wp-content/uploads/BFI_WP_201967.pdf.

16. Alison Gropnik and Tom Griffiths, "What Happens to Creativity as We Age?," *New York Times*, August 19, 2017, https://www.nytimes.com/2017/08/19/opinion/sunday/what-happens-to-creativity-as-we-age.html.

17. Bruce A. Weinberg and David W. Galenson, "Creative Careers: The Life Cycles of Nobel Laureates in Economics" (working paper 11799, National Bureau of Economic Research, November 2005).